DARTFORD TO SITTINGBOURNE

Vic Mitchell and Keith Smith

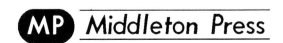
MP Middleton Press

First published July 1994

ISBN 1 873793 34 0

© Middleton Press 1994

Design - Deborah Goodridge

Published by Middleton Press
Easebourne Lane
Midhurst
West Sussex
GU29 9AZ
Tel: (0730) 813169
(From 16 April 1995 - (01730) 813169)

Printed & bound by Biddles Ltd,

CONTENTS

MAPS

ACKNOWLEDGEMENTS

So many of the photographers credited in the captions have given much additional information and for this we are extremely grateful. We are also appreciative of the assistance received from P.G.Barnes, R.M.Casserley, Chatham Historical Dockyard Museum, D.Collyer, Dr.E.Course, E.Crighton, G.Croughton, D.Hutson, N.Langridge, A.Ll.Lambert, J.S.Petley Mr.D.&Dr.S.Salter, G.T.V.Stacey, N.Stanyon, P.J.Tyrell and our ever helpful wives.

All maps are to the scale of 25" to 1 mile, unless otherwise stated. Diagrams and charts are not numbered.

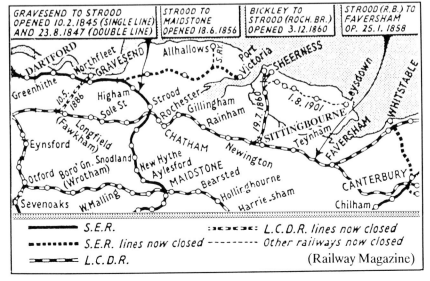

GRAVESEND TO STROOD OPENED 10.2.1845 (SINGLE LINE) AND 23.8.1847 (DOUBLE LINE)

STROOD TO MAIDSTONE OPENED 18.6.1856

BICKLEY TO STROOD (ROCH. BR.) OPENED 3.12.1860

STROOD (R.B.) TO FAVERSHAM OP. 25.1.1858

———— S.E.R.
••••••• S.E.R. lines now closed
⊂□⊃□⊂ L.C.D.R.
⋊⋉⋊⋉ L.C.D.R. lines now closed
-------- Other railways now closed

(Railway Magazine)

GEOGRAPHICAL SETTING

Dartford is an old established commercial and manufacturing centre situated at the first crossing point on the River Darent. The entire route is roughly parallel to the River Thames and is on the Chalk of the foot of the dip slope of the North Downs as far as Gravesend. This section is undulating owing to the number of dry valleys crossed.

The waterfront town of Gravesend was once a popular recreational resort, but this role declined towards the end of the last century. Reduction in the size of the Port of London brought less demand on the town's pilotage and towage services but it remains an important commercial centre and retains a ferry service across the Thames to Tilbury.

Hereafter the route traverses Shorne Marshes following closely the course of the former Thames & Medway Canal, the tunnel for which the railway now occupies between Higham and Strood. Emerging from this bore through Chalk, the line bridges the River Medway and passes through three short tunnels, again in Chalk, in the Rochester-Chatham conurbation. These towns have had a long maritime association, both mercantile and naval.

The remainder of the route to the paper manufacturing town of Sittingbourne is also on the dip slope of the North Downs and undulating in its final section.

The district between the Medway Towns and Sittingbourne was noted for its numerous brickyards.

The proximity of the raw materials for cement making (chalk and clay) to good transport (River Thames) resulted in the early development of this industry on a big scale in the Dartford-Strood area of the route. This concentration of works and their dust impact on the environment has led to the term White Country being applied, in contrast to the Midlands' Black Country.

Water transport has played the major role in the transport of materials for the cement and paper industries along the route, rail always being of lesser importance. Despite this, the route served the most industrialised area of the former Southern Railway.

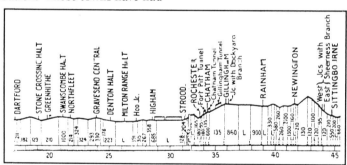

HISTORICAL BACKGROUND

The first railway in the area was the Gravesend & Rochester, a single line between the canal basins at Gravesend and at Strood. It opened on 10th February 1845 and ran parallel to the entire length of the Thames & Medway Canal, being built partly over it on stilts in the tunnels. These were eventually drained and infilled to allow double track to be brought into use on 23rd August 1847.

The South Eastern Railway commenced operating trains from London Bridge to Rochester (Strood) via Lewisham and Woolwich on 30th July 1849, the entire route from North Kent East Junction (north of Lewisham) coming into use that day. (The SER had purchased the Thames & Medway Canal and its associated railway). The line was extended up the Medway Valley to Maidstone on 18th June 1856.

The East Kent Railway started a service between Faversham and Chatham on 25th January 1858, offering a horse bus connection to the SER's Rochester station in Strood. The Chatham-Strood link was opened on 29th March of that year, after which date EKR coaches were attached to SER trains to and from London. Later that year the EKR changed its name to the London Chatham and Dover Railway and started to plan an independent route to the capital, via Bromley. This came into use on 3rd December 1860 and thereon the SER had a competitor instead of a supplier of traffic. The competition was taken to ludicrous lengths, most Kent towns of any size eventually being served by both companies.

LCDR trains began running between Sittingbourne and Sheerness on 19th July 1860 but the connection from the branch in the London direction did not come into use until about 1864.

Having lost most of the Rochester and Chatham traffic, the SER obtained an Act in 1881 for the construction of its own line across the Medway to these towns. Some ground was purchased but no other progress was made due to lack of funds. A fresh Act in 1888 resulted in the opening of a line to Rochester Common on 20th July 1891. On 1st March 1892 this was extended to a terminus called Chatham

Central, which was neither in Chatham nor central to it! The complexities of the resulting junction and train services are considered near pictures 45-58 in this album and also adjacent to pictures 109-111 in our *Bromley South to Rochester* album. The SER and LCDR were operated by a managing committee from 1st January 1899, the whole soon being known as the South Eastern & Chatham Railway. Despite this, the unnecessary Chatham Central branch lingered on until 1st October 1911.

The SECR became part of the Southern Railway in 1923. The SR soon embarked upon a comprehensive electrification programme which was implemented between Dartford and Gravesend on 6th July 1930 and between Gravesend and Gillingham on 2nd July 1939.

The SR became the Southern Region of British Railways upon nationalisation in 1948. The Gillingham-Sittingbourne part of the route was electrified as part of the Kent Coast electrification scheme on 15th June 1959.

PASSENGER SERVICES

West of Gillingham

The Gravesend & Rochester Railway had six trains per day, as did the Strood-Faversham section initially.

By 1869 there were eleven trains on weekdays from London to Strood, some continuing to Maidstone, and there were three extra as far as Gravesend. On Sundays ten trains ran to Strood or stations south thereof. A steamer ran from Strood Pier to Rochester and Chatham.

The 1878 timetable indicated nine trains to Maidstone, most having connections to Chatham. Additionally there were four to Gravesend, four to Strood and two through to Chatham. On Sundays there were seven journeys to Maidstone with no short workings.

The first timetable to include Chatham Central (1892) showed seven trains termed "Chatham Express" terminating there, plus connections from half of the 14 Maidstone trains. There were also a few short journeys. On Sundays the "Gravesend and Chatham Express" ran twice and there were seven Maidstone trains, some with connections to

Chatham Central.

By 1910 Chatham Central was served only by a railmotor making eleven trips on weekdays from Strood. A similar service had commenced between Dartford and Gravesend in 1906, making ten weekday journeys. In addition there were 15 trains from London to Maidstone, most having through coaches or connections to New Brompton (Gillingham) or beyond.

Further increases in service continued, a major change taking place in 1930 with the provision of a basic electric train timetable to Gravesend comprising three trains per hour, in addition to steam trains to stations further east. Electrification through to Gillingham in 1939 brought an hourly semi-fast train dividing at Strood for Maidstone, plus an hourly stopping train connecting at Strood for Maidstone.

After electrification to the Kent Coast in 1959, the basic timetable comprised an hourly service of three stopping trains to Gravesend, a Ramsgate/Maidstone service splitting at Strood and an all-stations to Gillingham.

The 1967 timetable indicated one Gravesend and two Gillingham trains each hour daily. Changes in 1976 increased local services to Gravesend to two, that frequency still applying in 1994, although not on Sundays.

East of Gillingham

The table below indicates the number of down services each day, but excludes boat trains and those operating less than five days per week.

	Weekdays	Sundays
1869	10	4
1878	9	3
1892	12	6
1910	15	5
1924	19	8
1930	22	7
1944	16	6
1954	27	25

There were two or three direct trains from Chatham to Sheerness each day until the mid-1930s after which time there were up to five. Following the formation of the SECR, a few trains east of Gillingham ran from London via the North Kent Line. For example, there were three in 1910 and six in 1924. Some of these gave direct services between the Naval towns of Greenwich, Woolwich, Chatham and Sheerness.

Electrification in 1959 provided a buffet car train from Victoria each hour which divided at Gillingham, the front portion running fast to Whitstable and on to Ramsgate, while the rear ran non-stop to Sittingbourne and terminated at Dover Priory. There was also an all-stations to Sheerness and a stopping train to Ramsgate each hour. Regular division at Gillingham ceased in 1967 but service frequency remained unchanged.

Hourly direct operation to Sheerness ceased in 1973, trains being redirected to Canterbury East. Division of fast trains at Gillingham recommenced at that time but there were still three trains per hour over the route, a frequency also applicable in 1994.

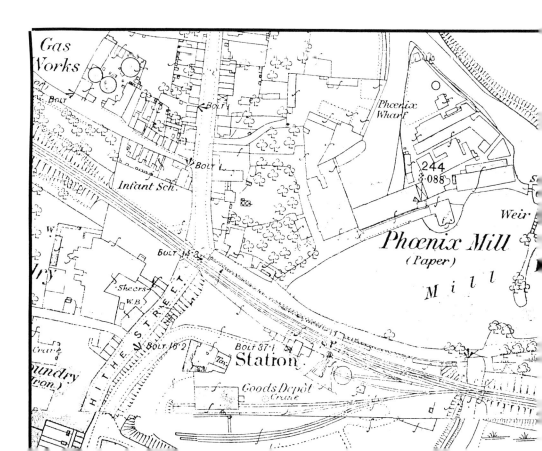

DARTFORD

1. The timber clad offices probably date from the opening of the line on 30th July 1849 but the brick built station house is thought to be of a later date. Both survived until 1972. (Lens of Sutton)

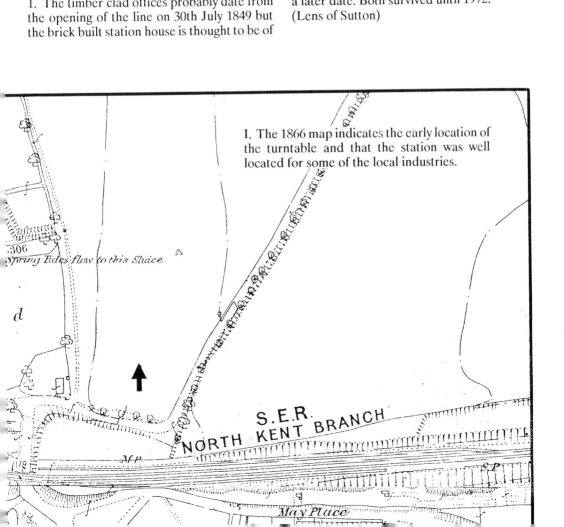

I. The 1866 map indicates the early location of the turntable and that the station was well located for some of the local industries.

.306
Spring Tides flow to this Sluice

d

S.E.R.
NORTH KENT BRANCH

May Place

2. A westward panorama in about 1910 includes the goods shed (left), No.2 Box (centre) and a locomotive obscuring the turntable, which is behind the signal box. (R.C.Riley coll.)

Other views of this station and later editions of the map can be found in the companion albums *Charing Cross to Dartford* **and** *Lewisham to Dartford* **in our London Suburban Railways Series.**

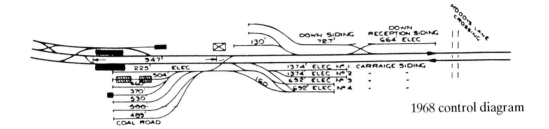

1968 control diagram

3. Electric services to London commenced in 1926 but only three platforms were available, the third (left) having been added in about 1897. The headcode indicates that the train is about to depart for Charing cross via Charlton and Blackheath. (Lens of Sutton)

4. An eastward view from the footbridge in April 1953 includes part of the goods yard but the down starting signals largely obscure the berthing sidings and No.2 Box, which remained in use until 8th November 1970. No.1 Box at the London end closed on 13th June 1954. (D.Cullum)

5. Class N1 2-6-0 no.31879 was recorded from the east end of platform 2 on 1st July 1957 while it was working a return Sunday excursion from the Thanet Coast to London. The shadow is that of the signals seen in the previous picture. (N.L.Browne)

6. A December 1965 photograph shows a mixture of mails, males and one female. All structures visible were demolished in the early 1970s to make way for a new station with four through platforms, which were fully commissioned on 5th August 1973. (J.N.Faulkner)

7. The rebuilding included a new footbridge and luggage lifts, as seen in this record of no.56065 proceeding with empties destined for Chatham Dockyard on 8th June 1991. All lines were signalled for reversible running and controlled by Dartford Panel. (V.Mitchell)

8. One mile east of the station the route has two reverse curves of about 30-chain radius which takes it closer to the Thames, which is visible above this engineers train on 12th December 1992. Also featured is no.47207 *Bulmers of Hereford*, the Queen Elizabeth II suspension bridge and the entrance to the Dartford Tunnel. This is below its tapered ventilation shafts. (B.Morrison)

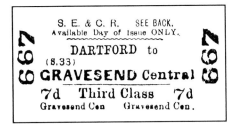

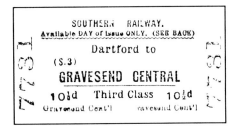

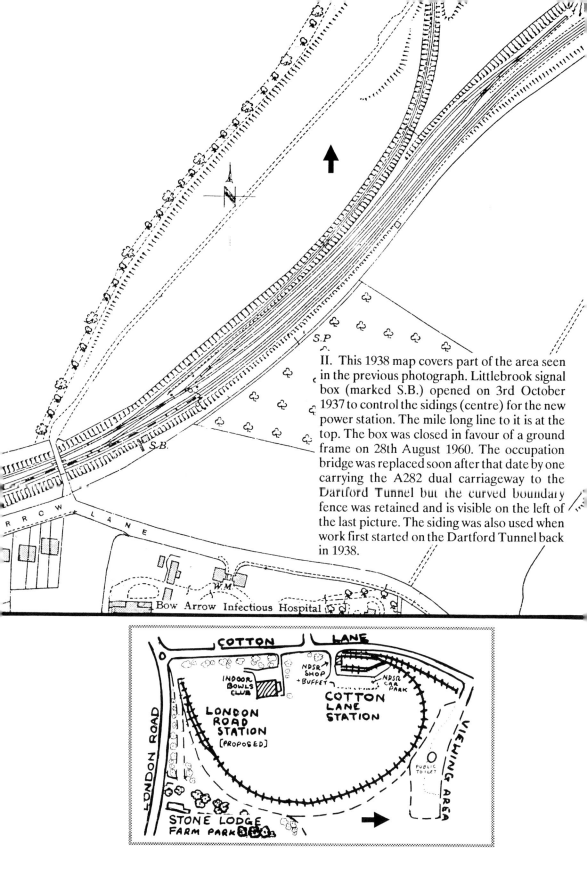

II. This 1938 map covers part of the area seen in the previous photograph. Littlebrook signal box (marked S.B.) opened on 3rd October 1937 to control the sidings (centre) for the new power station. The mile long line to it is at the top. The box was closed in favour of a ground frame on 28th August 1960. The occupation bridge was replaced soon after that date by one carrying the A282 dual carriageway to the Dartford Tunnel but the curved boundary fence was retained and is visible on the left of the last picture. The siding was also used when work first started on the Dartford Tunnel back in 1938.

S.P

S.B.

ARROW LANE

WM

Bow Arrow Infectious Hospital

COTTON LANE

NDSR SHOP + BUFFET

INDOOR BOWLS CLUB

NDSR CAR PARK

COTTON LANE STATION

LONDON ROAD STATION [PROPOSED]

LONDON ROAD

VIEWING AREA

PUBLIC TOILET

STONE LODGE FARM PARK

9. Established in 1980 to preserve part of the Gravesend West branch, the railway's stock moved to Stone in 1987 after occupying a number of sites mentioned in caption 44. This is Cotton Lane sidings in January 1993 with an ex-LT brake van, one of the company's two ex-Metropolitan Line T-stock coaches of 1932 and Ruston Hornsby no.1 *Scottie* in view. (NDSR)

10. Normally in use on the first and third Sunday of the month (except in January) is the railway's only operational steam locomotive, the 1955 Robert Stevenson & Hawthorn 0-6-0T *North Downs*. It is seen at Cotton Lane in November 1993, coupled to a van containing a diesel-powered compressor for train braking. This was attached to a recently acquired BR Mk 2 coach and a T-stock driving trailer. There were eight industrial diesel locomotives on site at that time, in addition to a number of items of freight stock and two bodies of ex-LCDR coaches. (NDSR)

STONE CROSSING

Deepwater Pier

Albion Portland
Cement Works

Shield Portland Cement
Works

Dolphins

Pier

Pier

Pier

Jetty

Greenhithe
Portland
Works

Stone

Watercress Bed

Watercress Bed

Watercress
Bed

F.B!

F.B!

Cotton Farm

B.M. 18·2

Artillery Cement Works

TRAMWAY

TRAMWAY

Whiting
Works

St. Mary's
Road

Brewery

Railway
Cottages

S.E. & C.R.
ORTH KENT LINE

25

Manorway
Place

M.P

Cotton Lane
Cottages

B.M. 76·2

Stone Court
Cottages

Lodge

The Orchard

Rectory

The Lawns

Chalk
Pit

Chalk Pit

F.P.

School

Church

Stone
Court

M. 121·2

Roman Pottery &
Human Remains
found A.D. 1906-7

Chalk Pit

50

100

Stone Place

Chalk Pit

Stone

100

121

Gravel Pit

Chichester
Lodge

Nightingale
Cottages

Sewage Filter

Cottage
Hospital

Horns Cross

London Bridge 17
Gravesend

M.S 124·3 G.P.

Barnesfield

B.M. 92·9

L.B

B.M. 125·6

120

F.O

Smy.

**CITY OF LONDON
MENTAL HOSPITAL**

Lodge

90

B.M. 102·4

G.P.

Stone
Park

B.M. 107·3

Stonelodge
Farm

110

Lodge

Hill
House

B.M. 92·9

Brick Works
(Disused)

Stone

Meth. Chap.

John's Hole

S **T** **O** **N** **E**

III. The 1910 edition at 6" to 1 mile does not
record the position of Stone Crossing Halt. It
is north of Stone, between the brewery and the
rectory. The map helps to locate the 25"
extracts following and serves to emphasise the
fact that so many of the industrial railways ran
to the Thames and not the North Kent Line.
The NDSR Cotton Lane station is now near
the chalk pit marked on the left of this map.

B.M. 153·9

St. Mary's Home
(Female Penitentiary)

Chap.

Lodge

B.M. 170·8

B.M. 180·4

The Hall

WATLING STREET

ROMAN ROAD

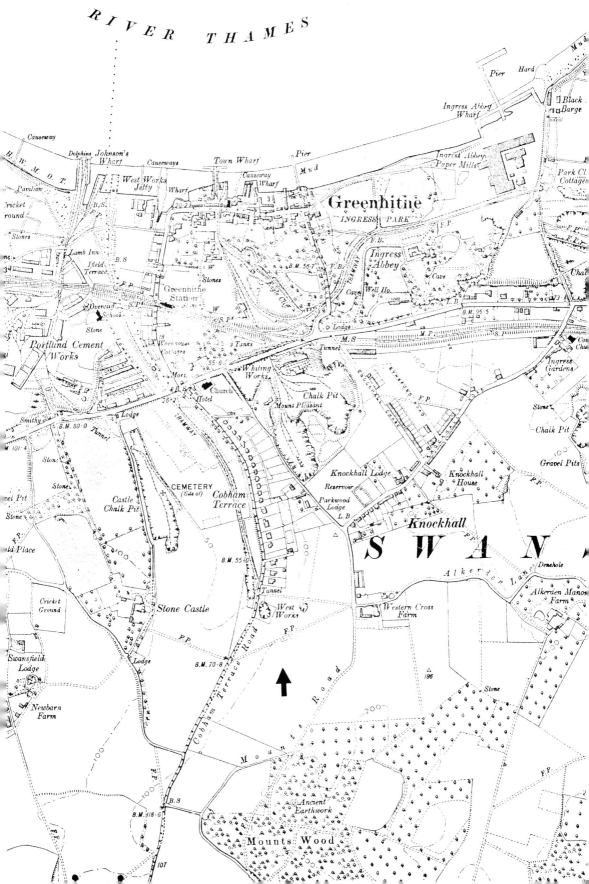

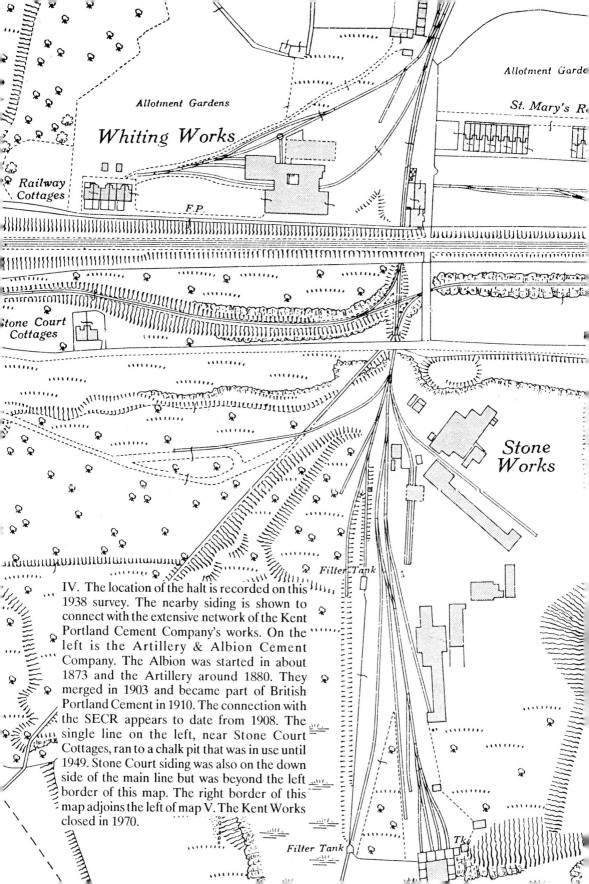

Allotment Gardens

Whiting Works

Allotment Garde

St. Mary's R

Railway
Cottages

F.P.

Stone Court
Cottages

Stone
Works

Filter Tank

IV. The location of the halt is recorded on this 1938 survey. The nearby siding is shown to connect with the extensive network of the Kent Portland Cement Company's works. On the left is the Artillery & Albion Cement Company. The Albion was started in about 1873 and the Artillery around 1880. They merged in 1903 and became part of British Portland Cement in 1910. The connection with the SECR appears to date from 1908. The single line on the left, near Stone Court Cottages, ran to a chalk pit that was in use until 1949. Stone Court siding was also on the down side of the main line but was beyond the left border of this map. The right border of this map adjoins the left of map V. The Kent Works closed in 1970.

Filter Tank

Tk

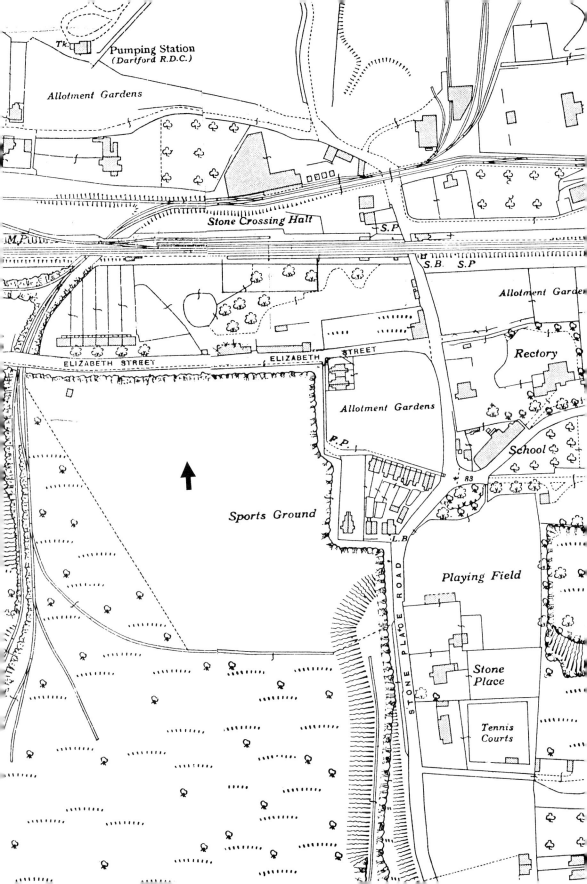

11. Stone Crossing Halt was opened on 2nd November 1908 when a railmotor (see picture 58 for an example) service was introduced between Dartford and Gravesend. This is the 11.19am New Cross to Ramsgate excursion on 11th July 1954, headed by class D1 no. 31741. Note the complex heading on the notice board. (D.Trevor Rowe)

12. An eastward view in 1969 includes the small signal box which was in use until 8th November 1970 when Dartford Panel took over its functions and colour light signals were introduced. It remained as a gate box and a source of tickets. (J.Scrace)

13. On 29th March 1978, the 14.12 Charing Cross to Gravesend via Eltham (Well Hall) was composed of class 415/1 4EPB no. 5033 and class 416/2 2EPB no. 5761. The EPBs were in terminal decline when this book was published in 1994 and the level crossing gates were still worked by hand. (B.Morrison)

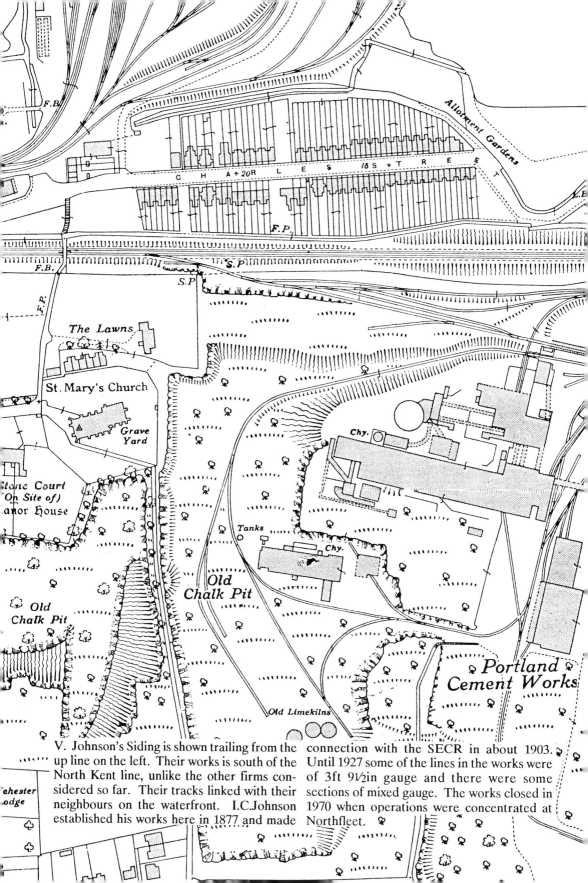

F.B.

Allotment Gardens

C H A + 20R L E S 16S + T R E E T

L.B.

F.P.

F.B.

S.P.

S.P.

F.P.

The Lawns

St. Mary's Church

Grave Yard

Chy.

...one Court
(On Site of)
...anor House

Tanks

Chy.

Old Chalk Pit

Old Chalk Pit

Portland Cement Works

Old Limekilns

V. Johnson's Siding is shown trailing from the up line on the left. Their works is south of the North Kent line, unlike the other firms considered so far. Their tracks linked with their neighbours on the waterfront. I.C.Johnson established his works here in 1877 and made connection with the SECR in about 1903. Until 1927 some of the lines in the works were of 3ft 9½in gauge and there were some sections of mixed gauge. The works closed in 1970 when operations were concentrated at Northfleet.

...chester
...odge

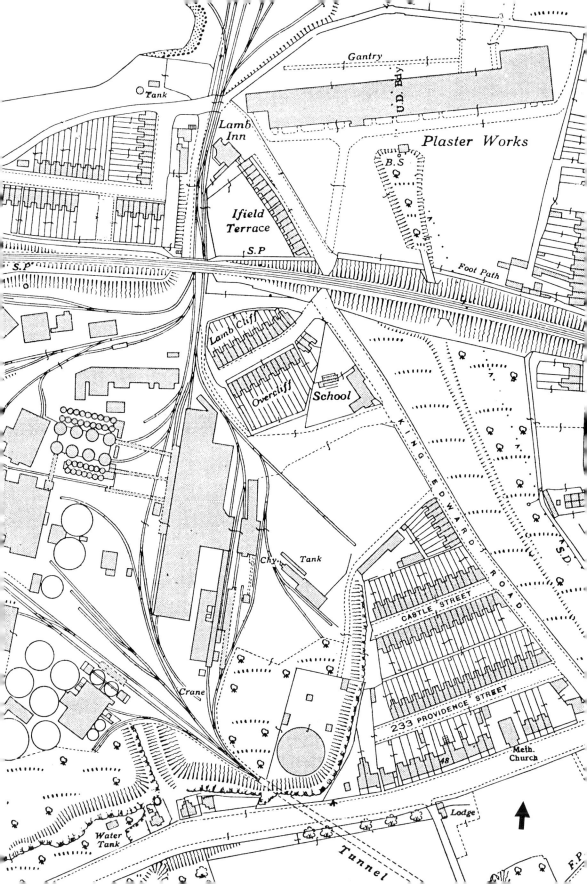

GREENHITHE

VI. On the left of this 1909 map, Johnson's tracks pass under the North Kent Line. To the right of the station are the lines of the Globe Portland Cement & Whiting Company. The works was in use from 1899 until 1920 approximately.

Dolphin

Dolphin

Johnson's Wharf

Causeway

M

u

West Works Jetty

Mud st.

B.S.

F.P.

Ground

ones

Stone

Lamb Inn

TRAMWAY

186 .477

B.S.

Ifield Terrace

W.M.

F.P.

S.P.

Lamb Cliff

Overcliff

School

TRAMWAY

Tank

Stone

KING EDWARD R?

land Cement

Works

14. The station opened with the line in 1849 but, while a substantial house was provided for the station master, there was no provision for goods traffic. The combined populations of Swanscombe and Greenhithe increased from 1763 in 1851 to 8494 in 1921. (Lens of Sutton)

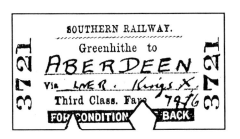

16. A 1968 westward view includes a cement works chimney but no signal box. The up distant was that of Stone Crossing which was almost one mile away. (J.N.Faulkner)

15. The signal box is included in the previous picture and was closed in July 1965. The "S" indicated the stopping position for all electric trains, regardless of their length.
(Lens of Sutton)

VII. Ingress Park Siding trails off the up line, crosses the down and is shown on the 1938 map, which has been reduced to 20" to 1 mile to include most of the Empire Paper Mills. The line opened in about 1919. Lower left is the 253yd long Greenhithe Tunnel.

Greenhithe

INGRESS

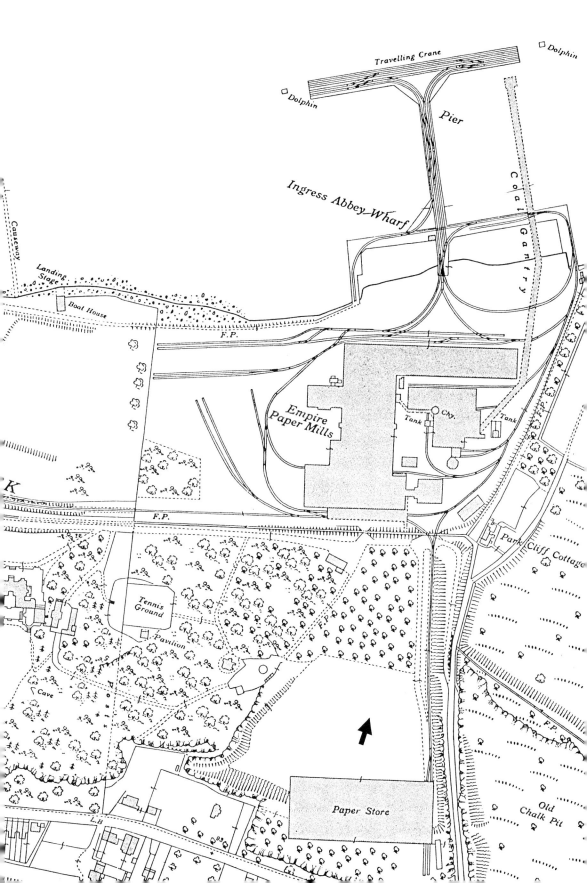

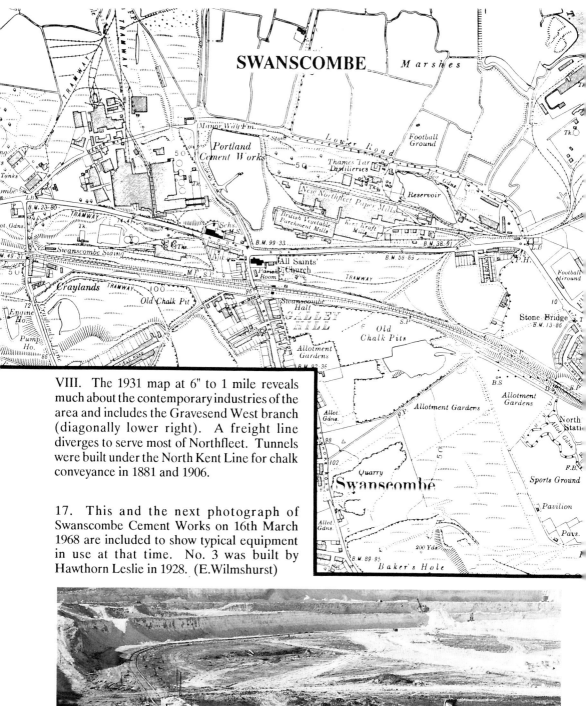

SWANSCOMBE

Marshes

VIII. The 1931 map at 6" to 1 mile reveals much about the contemporary industries of the area and includes the Gravesend West branch (diagonally lower right). A freight line diverges to serve most of Northfleet. Tunnels were built under the North Kent Line for chalk conveyance in 1881 and 1906.

17. This and the next photograph of Swanscombe Cement Works on 16th March 1968 are included to show typical equipment in use at that time. No. 3 was built by Hawthorn Leslie in 1928. (E.Wilmshurst)

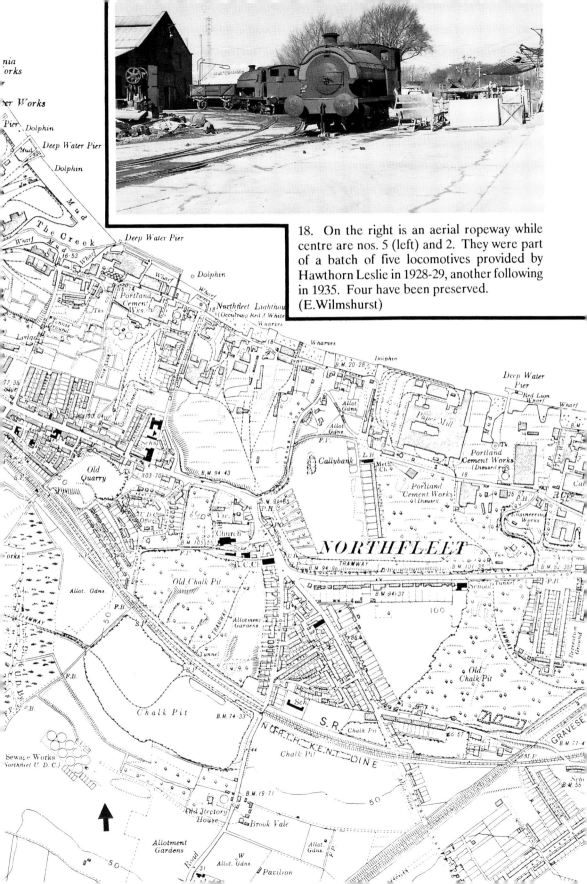

18. On the right is an aerial ropeway while centre are nos. 5 (left) and 2. They were part of a batch of five locomotives provided by Hawthorn Leslie in 1928-29, another following in 1935. Four have been preserved. (E.Wilmshurst)

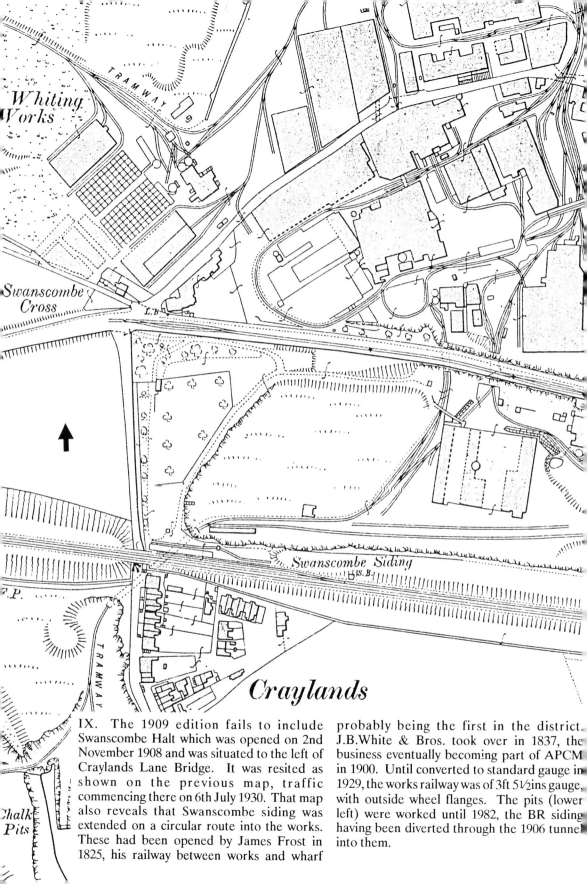

Whiting
Works

T R A M W A Y

Swanscombe
Cross

L.B.

Swanscombe Siding
IS.B.

T.P.

T R A M W A Y

Craylands

Chalk
Pits

IX. The 1909 edition fails to include Swanscombe Halt which was opened on 2nd November 1908 and was situated to the left of Craylands Lane Bridge. It was resited as shown on the previous map, traffic commencing there on 6th July 1930. That map also reveals that Swanscombe siding was extended on a circular route into the works. These had been opened by James Frost in 1825, his railway between works and wharf probably being the first in the district. J.B.White & Bros. took over in 1837, the business eventually becoming part of APCM in 1900. Until converted to standard gauge in 1929, the works railway was of 3ft 5½ins gauge, with outside wheel flanges. The pits (lower left) were worked until 1982, the BR siding having been diverted through the 1906 tunnel into them.

19. The transfer of the halt to this site in July 1930 would have brought it closer to the majority of residents in the locality. The suffix "Halt" was officially dropped by the Southern Region on 5th May 1969. (Lens of Sutton)

20. Unit 1530 passes under Swanscombe High Street on 6th July 1993, while working the 10.27 Charing Cross to Ramsgate service. A lamp post in the trees indicates the position of the access path. (J.Scrace)

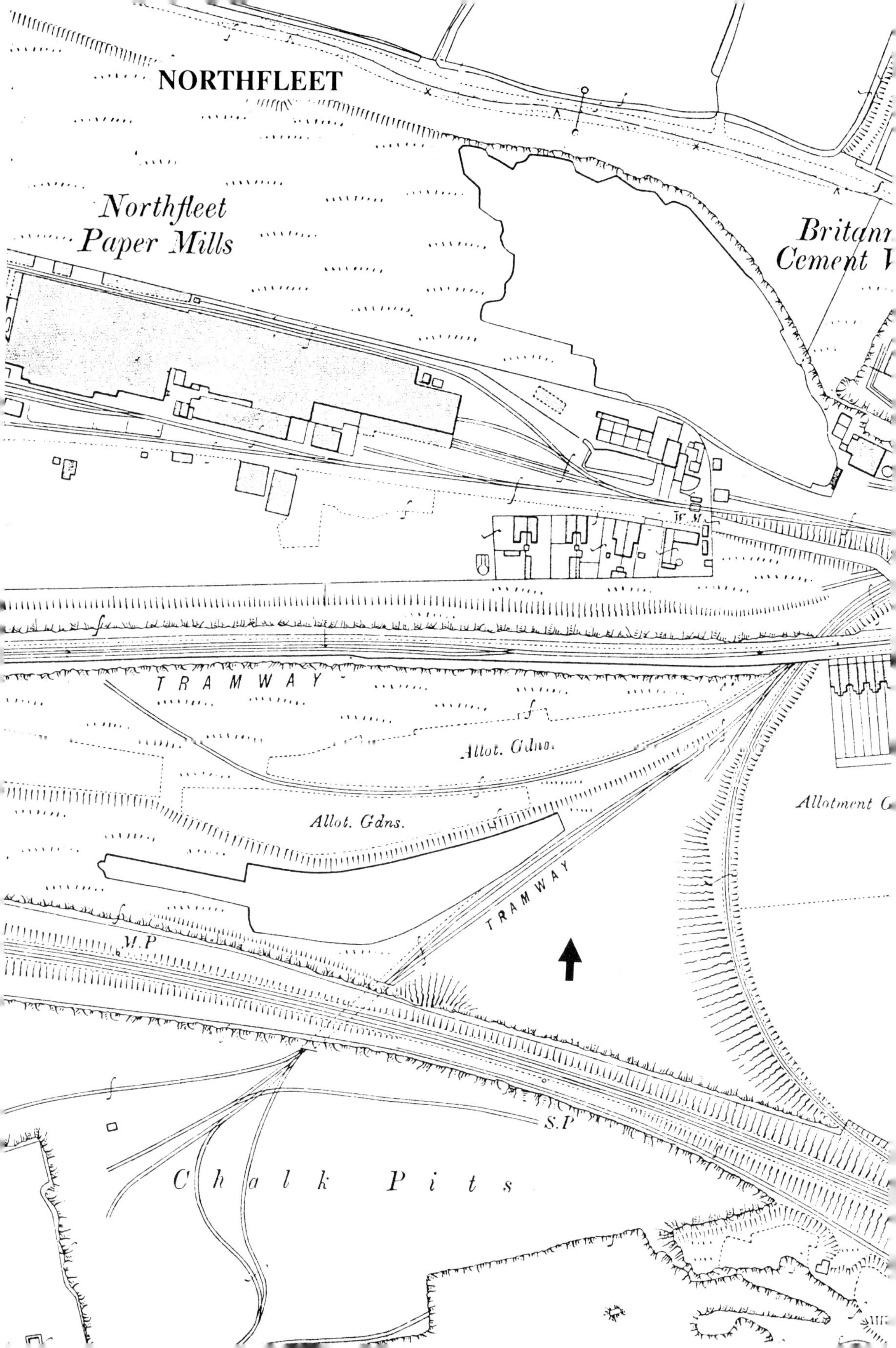

NORTHFLEET

Northfleet
Paper Mills

Britann
Cement W

W.M

T R A M W A Y

Allot. Gdns.

Allot. Gdns.

Allotment G

T R A M W A Y

M.P

S.P

C h a l k   P i t s

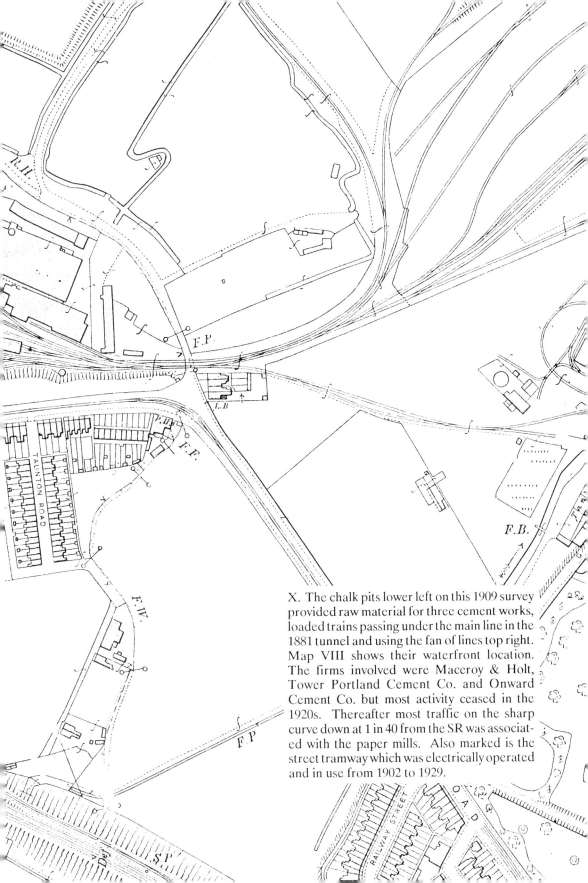

X. The chalk pits lower left on this 1909 survey provided raw material for three cement works, loaded trains passing under the main line in the 1881 tunnel and using the fan of lines top right. Map VIII shows their waterfront location. The firms involved were Maceroy & Holt, Tower Portland Cement Co. and Onward Cement Co. but most activity ceased in the 1920s. Thereafter most traffic on the sharp curve down at 1 in 40 from the SR was associated with the paper mills. Also marked is the street tramway which was electrically operated and in use from 1902 to 1929.

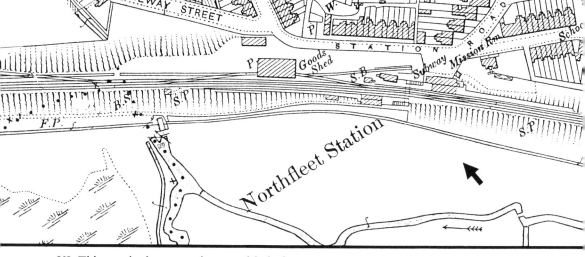

XI. This map is almost continuous with the last one but is the 1897 survey. On the left is a goods loop from which the cement works siding continues. More recently it has been known as Northfleet Deep Water siding.

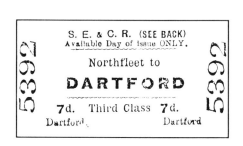

21. The architect for all the original stations from Dartford to Gravesend was Samuel Beazley but this example of his work was an early casualty, being demolished in 1891. The new buildings were erected east of the subway, the roof of which is on the right of this 1885 view. (Lens of Sutton)

22. The up side subway canopy and buildings were recorded in the 1960s when gas lights were still in use. The goods yard (right) closed on 9th September 1968, a 4½ ton capacity crane having been available for many years. (Lens of Sutton)

23. When pictured in 1969 the platforms had received new canopies and lights but the signal box retained its SER-style sash windows. The box was closed on 14th March 1971 when Dartford Panel took over. (J.Scrace)

24. Pylons and chimneys of cement works have for long been a feature of the White Country. A 2EPB unit passes the well kept station on 3rd November 1984. The population rose from 5000 in 1851 to 13000 in 1901, in round figures. (A.Dasi-Sutton)

25. The reason for this modest SER structure replacing the imposing brick and masonry building is not known. This 1993 view of the north elevation reveals that the chimneys have been removed. (J.Scrace)

26. Cement production commenced at a new works at Northfleet in 1970, the railway control room (left) coming into use on 14th December of that year. Above can be seen the canopy of Northfleet up platform as no. 33202 descends on the south side of the North Kent line embankment with gypsum from Mountfield on 3rd February 1987. On the right are two cripple sidings. Beyond the train are two reception and one departure road, together with a maintenance siding. (C.Wilson)

27. Turning round moments later we see no. 33202 passing under the main line bridge beyond which the track divides into two loops which rejoin the line on the left. The train will take the inner loop which first passes over the coal intake and then over the gypsum intake. The outer loop passes under the bulk cement silos where trains are loaded. The last gypsum train ran on 19th March 1993 and no cement has been despatched by rail since February of that year, all traffic being transferred to road despite Government rhetoric to the contrary. (C.Wilson)

28. An E class 4-4-0 speeds east in the summer of 1950 with a London to Allhallows excursion. It is passing under the Gravesend West branch which is fully illustrated in our *Bromley South to Rochester* album. (D.Trevor Rowe)

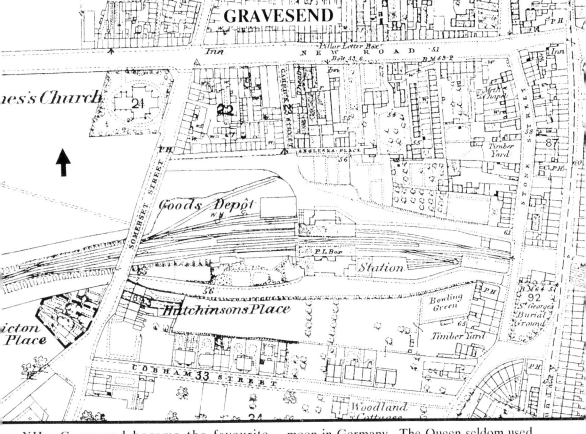

XII. Gravesend became the favourite embarkation point for Queen Victoria and the royal family when joining the Royal Yacht for visits overseas. On 2nd February 1858, a special train was run for the Princess Royal and her husband departing for their honey-moon in Germany. The Queen seldom used Dover and eventually abandoned Gravesend in favour of Port Victoria when it opened in September 1882 (see our *Branch Line to Allhallows*). This is the 1875 edition.

29. The station opened with the through route on 30th July 1849 and was recorded from the down platform 99 years later. Note that this was signalled for the starting of up trains and that one is disappearing in the distance. (Mowat coll.)

30. The station had been the terminus for electric trains from 1930 until 1939. This train of empty stock, shunted by class C no. 31112 on 2nd August 1954, is on the up through line. The far-sighted SER also provided two through tracks at Tonbridge, Paddock Wood and Ashford where fast trains were to be become more common. (F.Hornby)

31. H class 0-4-4Ts nos. 31517 and 31553 stand on the through roads on 3rd April 1960, the latter taking water between trips on the branch to Allhallows-on-Sea. The gaps in the conductor rails were for the safety of locomotive crews. (N.L.Browne)

32. The cramped goods yard was inadequate for the town which grew from 6700 folk in 1851 to over 14000 in 1921. The coming of the spacious yard at Gravesend West in 1886 resolved the problem. H class 0-4-4T no. 31308 is shunting on 25th November 1961. (A.E.Bennett)

33. The down platform "targets" display the words "Gravesend Central", a description that was in use from 1st July 1899 until 14th June 1965 although Gravesend West had closed to passengers on 3rd August 1953. (British Rail)

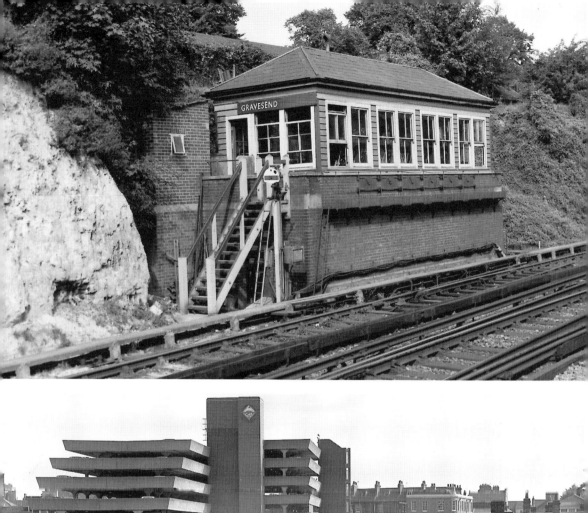

34. No. 2 Box had been at the east end of the station until 24th June 1928. Prior to that date, the box illustrated had been designated No. 1 and remained in use until 14th March 1971. This 1969 photograph includes the catch points of the electrified berthing siding which could also be used as a headshunt for the goods yard. (J.Scrace)

Branch Lines to Allhallows **contains other views of this station in pictures 1 to 8.**

36. Recorded on test on 6th July 1993 is one of the then new Networker trains, no. 466003 leading. The up platform (left) was used by most through trains by then, the down side being used for termination. The station was extensively refurbished in 1983. (J.Scrace)

35. The area on the right was the site of a locomotive turntable until the advent of electrification. A bay platform, often used by Allhallows trains between journeys, was built here subsequently. No. 56035 is working the 09.25 stone train from Grain to Hither Green on 16th September 1989. (A.Dasi-Sutton)

3rd· SINGLE SINGLE ·3rd
4655 (D.O) Gravesend Cen. to (D.O) 4655
Gravesend Cen.   Gravesend Cen
Denton Halt   Denton Halt
DENTON HALT
(S) 4d·H   FARE   4d·H (S)
For Conditions see over For Conditions see over

DENTON

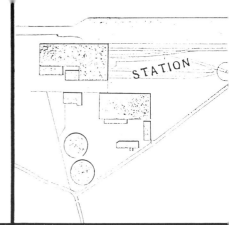

XIII. The 1852 plan (right) indicates the relationship of the terminus of the Gravesend & Rochester Railway to the canal and the gasworks shown on the map below, which is from 1869. The station was in use only from 1845 until 1849. The basin is now used by pleasure craft.

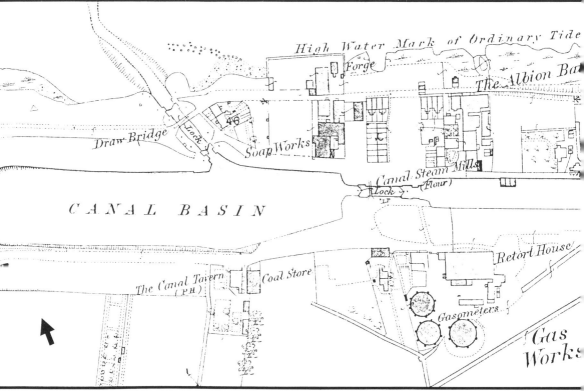

37. Denton Halt was a little over one mile from Gravesend and was in use from 1st July 1906 until 4th December 1961. Mid-way between the two was Milton Road Halt which opened on the same day but closed on 1st May 1915. Concrete platforms and gas lighting were provided in 1954. (A.E.Bennett)

38. The Thames & Medway Canal opened in 1824 and provided a short and direct link between the two rivers for sailing barges and avoided the long circumnavigation of the Isle of Grain. The western half remained in use until the 1920s for local agricultural traffic and raw materials from the Ural Mountains to the Uralite Works. About a one mile length still remains, although overgrown with reeds. The drawbridge by Trees Crossing was photographed in 1974 and restored to working order in 1994, by which time the canal had been cleared westward. (D.Cullum)

MILTON RANGE HALT

39. The halt was in use from 1st July 1906 until 17th July 1932 for scheduled traffic and by arrangement thereafter. It was still extant in 1994. On 21st August 1922, three deaths resulted from the collision of class B1 4-4-0 no. 457 (centre) with a workmans train standing at the halt. The driver of the B1, which was right-hand drive, had left Gravesend against the starting signal. The train in the background was not involved. (Lens of Sutton)

HOO JUNCTION

40. At the end of the 1956 Staff Halt are the junction signals for the line to Grain, part of the branch that once went to Allhallows-on-Sea. A Gillingham to Charing Cross train was recorded on 13th May 1971, along with some of the posts that once supported overhead electrification wires. The up platform is out of sight, beyond the water tank. (M.J.Furnell)

Yard diagram for December 1993.

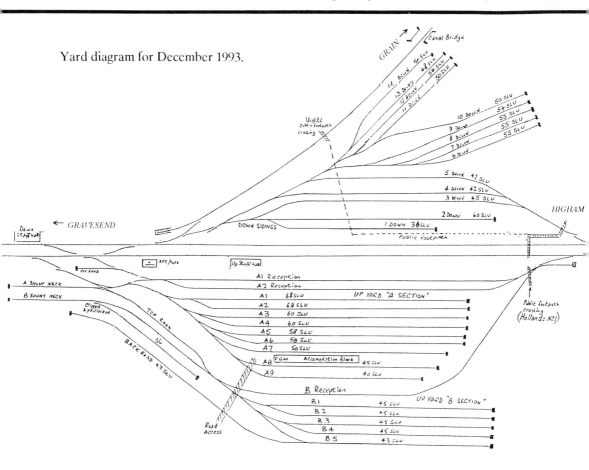

HIGHAM

41. Now the oldest station on the route, having opened with the G&RR in 1845, it initially served a community of about 800 souls which took 70 years to double. Note the trap-door and steps in the up platform. (SR Magazine)

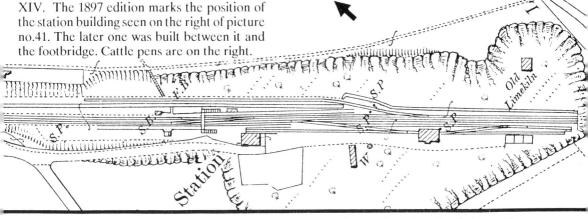

XIV. The 1897 edition marks the position of the station building seen on the right of picture no.41. The later one was built between it and the footbridge. Cattle pens are on the right.

42. A westward view includes wagons in the refuge siding (right). Charles Dickens was a regular user of this station as he lived nearby. Goods traffic continued until 4th September 1961, the goods shed having a 30 cwt crane. (Lens of Sutton)

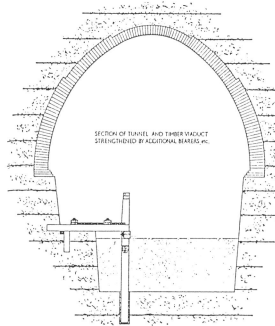

SECTION OF TUNNEL AND TIMBER VIADUCT
STRENGTHENED BY ADDITIONAL BEARERS etc.

43.   Behind the signal box, which closed on 17th October 1971, is a bridge carrying a footpath which passes over the siding and up steps in the wall of the cutting. The bridge is over a ditch which is the remnant of the canal. Having been built for a canal, the tunnels are level and therefore present drainage problems. Built as one tunnel 3946 yd long, it was opened out in 1830 to provide a passing place for boats. Higham Tunnel is now 1531 yd in length and Strood Tunnel is 2329.
(Lens of Sutton)

44.   The North Downs Steam Railway leased the goods yard site from 1981 until 1983 as a temporary depot during its quest for a permanent site. Before moving to Stone near Dartford, it obtained accommodation in Chatham Dockyard and then at Cory's Wharf in Rochester. The south and west elevations were photographed in July 1988. Although all the windows were boarded up the booking office was still in use in 1994, although only on weekday mornings. (J.Scrace)

STROOD

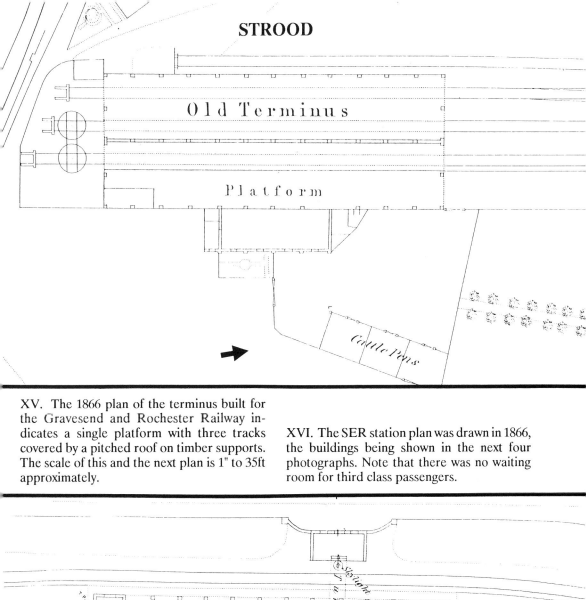

XV. The 1866 plan of the terminus built for the Gravesend and Rochester Railway indicates a single platform with three tracks covered by a pitched roof on timber supports. The scale of this and the next plan is 1" to 35ft approximately.

XVI. The SER station plan was drawn in 1866, the buildings being shown in the next four photographs. Note that there was no waiting room for third class passengers.

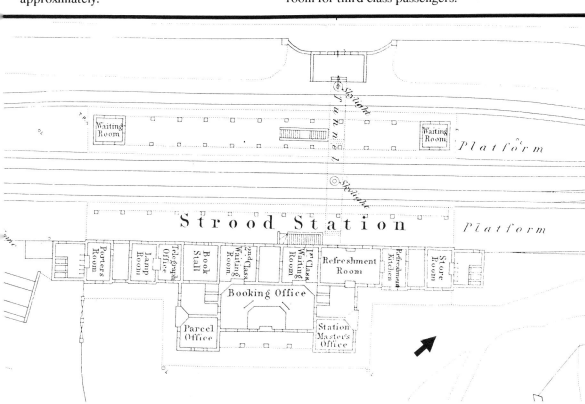

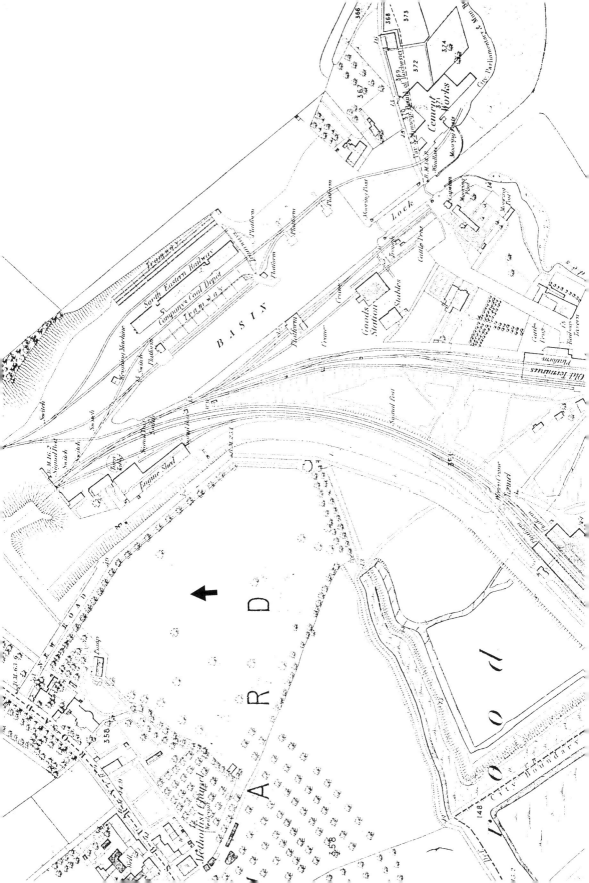

XVII. Strood Tunnel is on the left, in line with the basin and lock which it once served. Near the mouth of the tunnel is the SER's engine shed and turntable. Near the top of this 1866 map is a rail-served cement works and below it the "Old Terminus" is marked. This was in use from 10th February until 18th June 1856, when the station below it and the line to Maidstone was opened. Running across the bottom of the map is the LCDR's London to Chatham line of 1860. The connecting spur opened on 29th March 1859. Also marked (bottom right) is the LCDR's "Strood Station", which had been renamed "Rochester Bridge" on 1st April 1861, "Rochester & Strood" on 1st November 1861, "Rochester Bridge (Strood)" in 1862 and "Rochester Bridge" in 1905. On the right, the road and rail bridges are shown to incorporate draw bridges, although the latter was in fact a swing bridge. Close to it is a flour mill worked by tidal power from the large mill pond marked nearby.

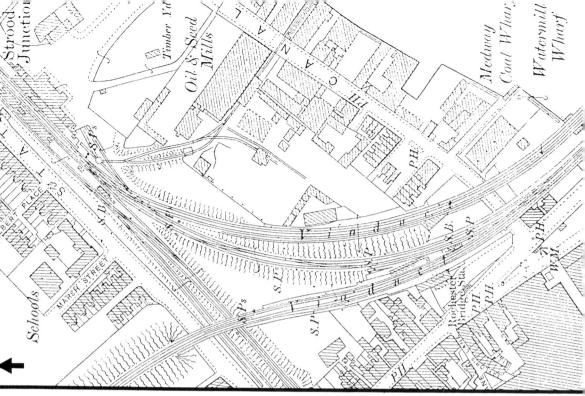

XVIII. The 1909 edition includes the stations and lines marked on the previous map but also shows a third bridge across the Medway, that built by the SER for its Chatham Central branch. The line passed over the site of the flour mill. The connecting spur between the LCDR and SER ceased to carry passenger trains in 1860 when the LCDR commenced direct running to London. This deprived passengers between the North Kent and the Medway towns of a direct link. After prolonged campaigning, a service was resumed on 1st April 1877 as a result of Mayor Toomer of Rochester taking the dispute before the Railway Commissioners. Subsequently his name was attached to the connecting spur, it being dubbed the "Toomer Loop".

46. Although more spacious than most SER stations, it was constructed economically with timber as were many later SER stations. Photographed in 1914, the structure was replaced by a flat-roofed CLASP design in 1973. (D.Cullum coll.)

45. This photograph was dated September 1854 and was taken before the completion of the western entrance to the subway and the infilling of the watercourse in the foreground to allow the building of New Road, now Station Road. The presence of signals suggests that the station might have been used as a terminus prior to the opening of the line to Maidstone. (Lens of Sutton)

47. The station had been scheduled for replacement at the time of electrification in 1939 but this was delayed due to the advent of war. On the right of this 1914 view is a grounded coach body of some antiquity. (D.Cullum coll.)

48. A down train is signalled to cross Rochester Bridge on 28th May 1938. At this time there were two through trains on weekdays between Gillingham and Brighton which reversed here and at Tonbridge. The locomotive on the right is H class 0-4-4T no. 1278 and on the left is R class 0-4-4T no. 1669. (H.C.Casserley)

49. Viewed from the down platform on 23rd May 1959 is an up Victoria express passing over the Maidstone line and the two electrified berthing sidings. The bridge had been reconstructed in 1927 in a new position in line with the SER bridge over the Medway and to a higher specification to take the heavier locomotives then being introduced. (A.E.Bennett)

50. The railway-owned Strood Dock is evident as C class nos. 31717 and 31267 approach the tunnel with empty stock from Gillingham to Rotherhithe Road on 4th June 1960. Earlier that day, the train had conveyed 700 Sea Scouts from Cannon Street to Chatham Dockyard.

51. In the street on the right of the picture, there used to be a public house named "The Amalgamation", which celebrated (inaccurately) the coming together of the LCDR and the SER. When photographed in March 1966,

This view from Strood Tunnel box includes the brickwork of the former turntable pit. In 1938, the goods yard was recorded as having a 15-ton crane while the dock sidings had a 6-ton model. The dock has recently been infilled.
(J.J.Scrace)

platform 1 was still the point at which down electric trains were divided. The front portion ran to Maidstone West while the rear coaches continued to Gillingham. (J.N.Faulkner)

52. A class 73 electro-diesel emerges from Strood Tunnel on 30th November 1970 while an up train stands at platform 2. Goods facilities at Strood Dock ceased on 1st November 1962 but the goods yard remained open until 16th August 1971 for general traffic. Coal and china clay were handled exclusively thereafter. Coal for Kingsnorth Power station was unloaded until 15th January 1986. Back in 1931 the dock sidings had handled 55000 tons of traffic, mainly coal, fertilisers and stone. Only a heap of rubble remains of the recently demolished engine shed. Originally having only a single road, this was doubled by the SER so that it could house 18 locomotives. It closed in 1939 and was subsequently used as a goods shed. (M.J.Furnell)

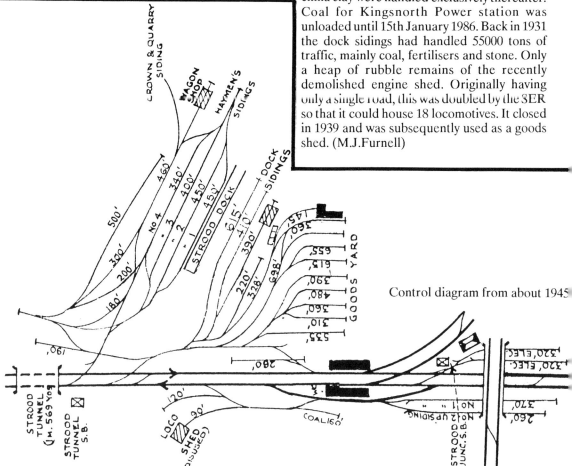

Control diagram from about 1945

53. Tunnel Box (left) and Junction Box (left in picture no. 49) both opened in the early weeks of 1939 and closed together on 17th October 1971. Here we see the 17.35 Cannon Street to Strood leaving the tunnel on 13th May 1971. (M.J.Furnell)

54. Known as "Strood Junction" for many years, the station is seen from the ex-LCDR line on 10th April 1993. By then all trains from Maidstone West terminated in the loop platform on the left. Prior to electrification all up trains from the Medway Valley ran through that platform. Gatwick Airport was the destination of some Medway line services starting here from May 1994. (V.Mitchell)

Other pictures and maps of this interesting station can be found in our companion album *Strood to Paddock Wood.*

ROCHESTER BRIDGE

55. The former LCDR Rochester Bridge station is on the left in this westward view from April 1933. On the right are the arches erected by the SER prior to 1892, the locomotive being on the curve from Strood station. The Toomer Loop was removed following the closure of Chatham Central in 1911. It had used the tapering span (left of centre) prior to the erection of the signal box. (L.Catchpole)

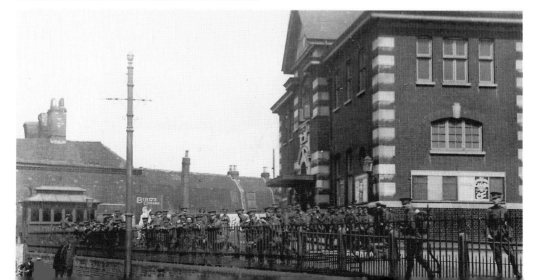

56. The imposing 1908 building faced south on to the main road and is also visible on the left of the main picture. It was wartime economies which brought about the closure of the station on 1st January 1917. These troops were recorded here on 6th August 1914.
(Lens of Sutton)

57. A 1933 eastward view has the ex-SER bridge on the left, this carrying all rail traffic from 29th June 1919 following a fire on the adjacent bridge. This necessitated revival of the Toomer Loop until 8th January 1922. The ex-LCDR bridge (centre) ceased to be used in 1927 when the new junction signal box, seen in picture 56, came into use. From 1912 until 1927, the routes had converged at the east end of the bridges. During World War II the centre

bridge was made available as an alternative to the adjacent bridges in the event of either being damaged. Rails were laid and timber fixed level with them for use by road vehicles, but the emergency never arose. The bridge was subsequently dismantled and its abutments now carry a new road bridge. The road bridge shows limits of 16 tons and 8 mph. (L.Catchpole)

CHATHAM CENTRAL

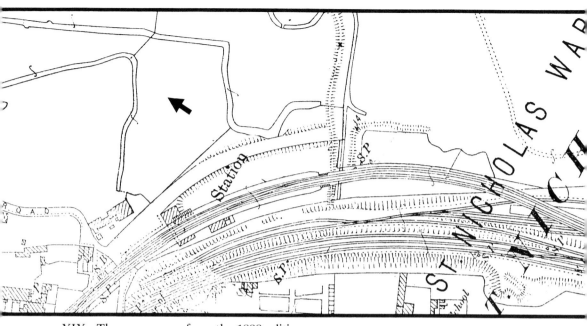

XIX. These maps are from the 1898 edition. The upper one includes the SER Rochester Common station which was a terminus from 20th July 1891 to 1st March 1892. It also shows the LCDR connection from its main line down to the goods yard, which involved a reversal. The lower map shows the continuation of the goods yard and the remainder of the SER branch to Chatham Central. Near the centre is the LCDR station which had only two platforms at that time. On the right is Fort Pitt Tunnel (428 yds long) and the line to Chatham.

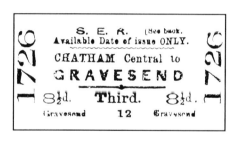

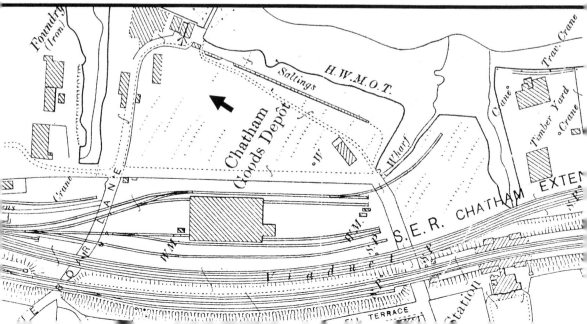

58. This is the only known photograph of Chatham Central which had three tracks, one platform and closed on 1st October 1911. It was the end of one of the most expensive and unnecessary railways in Britain, which had been built on a viaduct across the LCDR goods yard. The yard had been completed by 1886, allegedly to create an obstruction to the SER line. (Lens of Sutton)

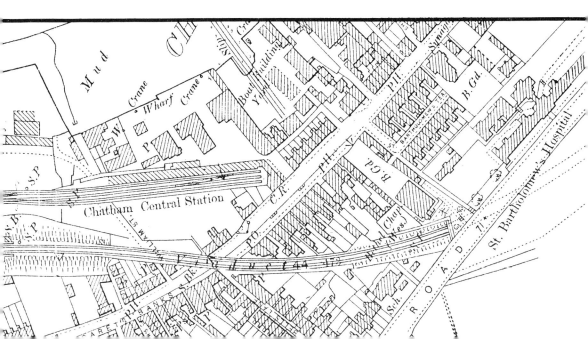

ROCHESTER

59. This, and the next two photographs, were taken on 28th June 1902 and show the situation before the quadrupling and provision of four platforms in 1911. The station had opened on 1st March 1892. SECR no. 460 was supplied by Sharp Stewart to the LCDR in 1861. It was initially named *Brigand* and was eventually withdrawn in 1903. (K.Nunn/LCGB)

60. Ex-SER Q class 0-4-4T no. 368 is working an up train on the 27 chain reverse curves between Fort Pitt tunnel and the station. The LCDR used lattice signal posts in common with the LSWR. In 1931 the station handled all mail traffic for the Medway towns - 330,935 bags in and 217,909 out. There were also 9200 milk churns received that year.
(K.Nunn/LCGB)

61. On the right we see a timber signal post on the SER Chatham Central line while SECR G class 4-4-0 no. 677 passes with the 3.20pm from Victoria. The line on the left was slewed to the left to become the up loop, most of the widening taking place on the right following the demolition of the SER brick viaduct. (K.Nunn/LCGB)

Control diagram showing the wartime tracks across the former LCDR bridge connected at the east end only.

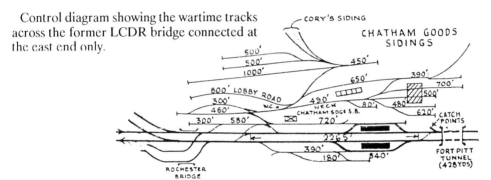

62. Platform covering was generous although many trains did not stop here. The four tracks were of value in providing the only passing place for many miles in all three directions, except at congested Chatham. Rochester has for long attracted visitors to its historic cathedral and castle, both of which are visible in picture no. 52. (D.Cullum coll.)

63. The 3.26pm Victoria to Ramsgate is running through on Sunday 26th July 1953, headed by class L no. 31776. Work was in progress on platform and canopy improvements. (N.Sprinks)

SINGLE   SINGLE -2nd

Rochester to

Rochester
Stone Crossing Halt
etc.

Rochester
Farningham Road
etc.

FARNINGHAM ROAD or
STONE CROSSING HALT

(S)   4/0   Fare   4/0   (S)
For conditions see over   For conditions see over

1288   1288

64. Class Q1 no.33034 heads an up freight from Chatham Goods on 3rd June 1959. The rear wagons are crossing the down line while the brake van is still on the goods loop. Close to it is Rochester signal box, the panel of which came into use on 10th May of that year. Beyond is Chatham Goods Sidings box which had closed the previous day. At a low level on the left are wagons in the goods yard which was in use until July 1988. It was subsequently used for wagon storage. (J.J.Smith)

65. The south elevation of the original LCDR station is seen in 1991 when the basic service comprised two stopping trains to both Victoria and Charing Cross each hour. Two years later, two fast trains to Victoria called each hour as well. The rails are level with the upper windows. (J.Scrace)

66. One of the first visits of Networker class 465 units was recorded on 19th January 1993, while on trial. At that time the loop lines were normally only used at peak times. The train is on the up through line. (M.Turvey)

CHATHAM

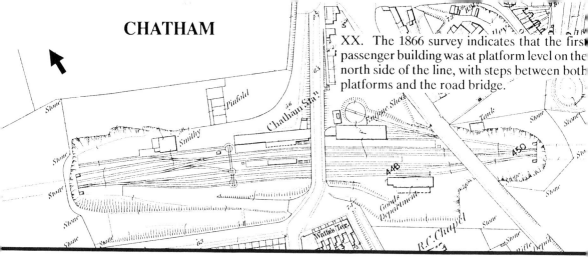

XX. The 1866 survey indicates that the first passenger building was at platform level on the north side of the line, with steps between both platforms and the road bridge.

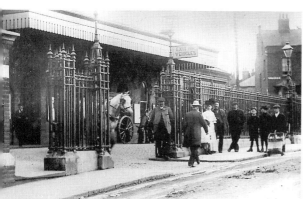

67. The station opened on 25th January 1858 as a terminus of the line from Faversham, passengers for London continuing by road to join an SER train on the other side of the Medway. Through coaches ran from March 29th of that year but this high level entrance came into use later. (Lens of Sutton)

68. A view from above Fort Pitt Tunnel includes the four through passenger platforms, a mail and parcels platform (left) and the military platform and dock on the right. The picture emphasises the congested layout. (Lens of Sutton)

69. A Gillingham to Allhallows train emerges from Chatham Tunnel behind class R 0-4-4T no.1665. Two or three such push-pull trains reversed at Hoo Junction on weekdays for most of the 1930s.
(D.H.Wakely/J.R.W.Kirkby)

70. Q class 0-6-0 no.30544 runs through non-stop on 26th July 1953 with the 11.17am Sunday excursion from Bromley South to Sheerness-on-Sea. The signal box was designated "A" until 1933 and was in use until 10th May 1959 when Rochester Panel took over. For many years there had been a siding on the right of this view for Elders & Fyffe's banana traffic. The crossed searchlight signals came into use on 16th May 1954. (N.Sprinks)

XXI. The 1932 map shows the later position of the goods shed (north of the platforms) and main entrance (on the bridge). It also reveals the position of "B" Box (right) which closed on 26th February 1933.

71. The booking hall is seen in the 1950s, soon after the price of platform tickets had been doubled to 2d. This was (and is) one of the busiest stations on the route. In 1931 it issued 380,413 tickets and handled over 96,000 parcels. A new booking hall was opened on 6th June 1981. (British Rail)

72. A military lorry is on the dock as class N15 no 30799 *Sir Ironside* blows off on 4th September 1958. Conductor rails can be seen on all sidings and running lines. (P.Hay)

73. The 2.9pm Victoria to Dover Priory was composed of seven coaches and class L no.31779 on 13th June 1959. At this time the platforms were lengthened for 12-coach electric trains, this necessitating the abolition of the loops and sidings. Part of the space gained on the up side has been used for a buffet and large waiting room. (J.J.Smith)

74. Between the 297yd long Chatham Tunnel and the 897yd Gillingham Tunnel the route climbs at 1 in 135 on a 28-chain curve over the three Luton Arches. No.3157 is one of a pair of class 423 units working the 10.23 Victoria to Dover Priory service on 3rd September 1988. (B.Morrison)

GILLINGHAM

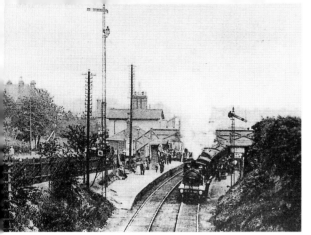

75. Opened as "New Brompton" on an unrecorded date in 1858, the station became "New Brompton (Gillingham)" in 1886, "Gillingham" in 1912 and "Gillingham (Kent)" in 1923. The district grew rapidly from about 9000 souls in 1851 to 42000 fifty years later. (Lens of Sutton)

76. The level crossing east of the station is seen on 19th July 1958 as no.30793 *Sir Ontzlake* departs for the Kent Coast. The end of the locomotive shed is on the left. (D.Trevor Rowe)

XXII. The Dockyard branch is at the top of this 1898 map onto which the later signal boxes have been marked. The original box is near the branch junction (S.B.)

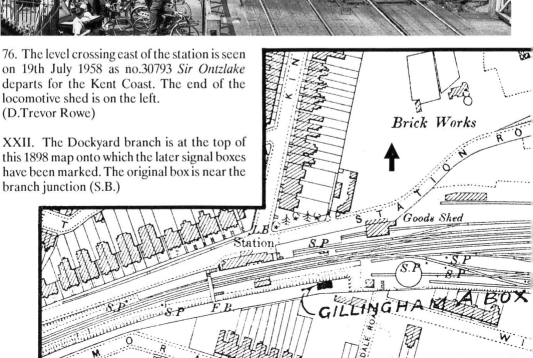

77. A new entrance, footbridge and down platform canopy were provided in 1932 but the old house is evident as "Schools" class no.30916 *Whitgift* stands adjacent to it on 19th July 1958. (A.E.Bennett)

78. Known as "B" Box until it took over the work of "A" Box on 21st January 1973, this box had controlled full lifting barriers since 21st June 1964. Class 411/5 4CEP no.1521 is proceeding to Gillingham Depot on 19th October 1990 while no.33046 waits on the Chatham Dockyard branch. (B.Morrison)

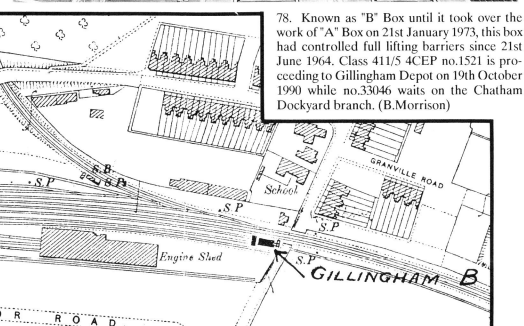

79. The 1932 improvements are shown in detail as unit no.465241 terminates, having left Charing Cross at 13.57. Unit 1547 forms the 13.54 Ramsgate to Victoria. (J.Scrace)

80. The 1932 entrance was recorded in 1993. It was built on a bridge over the tracks and an up island platform was provided at this time. Work started in 1993 on a solid state interlocking signalling centre which would control a large part of North Kent. Its area was planned to range to Farningham Road, Newington, Woolwich Arsenal, Falconwood and Beltring. (J.Scrace)

GILLINGHAM DEPOT

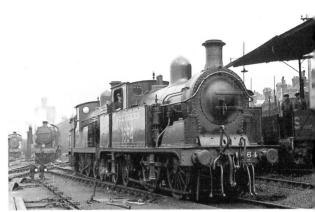

81. The three-road shed dates from 1885 when it was built in brick, with a slate roof. By 1898, there were 25 drivers on the roster. Class B1 no.1448 is featured on 4th February 1934. (H.C.Casserley)

82. Portrayed on 28th May 1938 is class R no.1664. The roof over the coal dock was added in 1931. The locomotive allocation was halved following electrification in 1939. (H.C.Casserley)

83. One of the new electric trains stands in the wings as part of the locomotive fleet fill the stage on 9th July 1939, their last full summer season. From left to right are class E no.1176, O1 no.1064, C no. 1234 and O1 no. 1003. (W.A.Camwell)

84. A snap from an eastbound train on 12th November 1949 includes the 50ft turntable bearing R class no.1662 and in the centre of the view is B1 class no.1441. (J.R.W.Kirkby)

85. Recent platform lengthening is included in this photograph from 1959. The 1955 coaling gantry enabled coal to be moved across several tracks. The few remaining engines were transferred to Tonbridge in 1959 and the site was sold for industrial purposes. (J.J.Smith)

86. Moving east, beyond the engine sheds, we see the electric reception roads and a train entering the washing plant. The photograph was taken from the same footbridge as picture no.78, but in the opposite direction. No.34080 *74 Squadron* is working an up relief train on 19th April 1954. (S.C.Nash)

87. From the same viewpoint as the previous picture, we observe an unusual formation. Two MLVs (Motor luggage vans) haul two tankers to London Bridge on 29th March 1991, prior to the Gala Weekend there. By then the reception roads had been provided with walkways. (A.Dasi-Sutton)

88. After passing along the reception roads, trains reverse into one of the four shed roads or adjacent three sidings. Most units visible on 7th July 1991 were of the nearly obsolete 4EPB type. (M.J.Stretton)

CHATHAM DOCKYARD

89. Map XXII shows the commencement of the branch which is seen to the right of an electro-diesel class 73 and a class 09 diesel shunter stabled in a siding on Saturday 16th May 1992. The 09 and van worked the Sheerness-Ridham Dock scrap steel trains, except at weekends. (V.Mitchell)

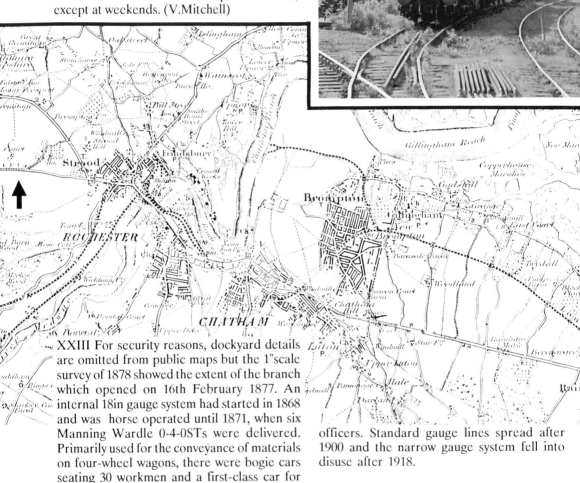

XXIII For security reasons, dockyard details are omitted from public maps but the 1"scale survey of 1878 showed the extent of the branch which opened on 16th February 1877. An internal 18in gauge system had started in 1868 and was horse operated until 1871, when six Manning Wardle 0-4-0STs were delivered. Primarily used for the conveyance of materials on four-wheel wagons, there were bogie cars seating 30 workmen and a first-class car for officers. Standard gauge lines spread after 1900 and the narrow gauge system fell into disuse after 1918.

Some indication of the extent of the system was given on a 1947 Admiralty navigation chart. Gillingham station is lower right. The largest building on the left housed covered slips for all-weather ship building or repair. The loops on the right served the coal yard, vast tonnages being required by ships in the pre-oil era.

90. The 4.0pm special for sea scouts waits to leave the branch on 18th May 1959, Whit Monday. Train engine is no.31495, pilot is no.31721 and at the rear is no.31720, all of class C. Class N no.31827 hauled the train to London Bridge. The train had come down on the previous Saturday and been berthed for two nights at Rainham. The locomotive depot, water tank and coaling plant are all visible. (J.J.Smith)

91. Few photographs were taken inside these secure premises. This one from the 1950s includes an Andrew Barclay 0-4-0ST at work at the east end of No.3 Basin. (A.Bruce)

92. Railtours have occasionally traversed the branch, this one being recorded on 24th September 1960 behind no. D3721 and H class 0-4-4T no.31177. Kent County councillors had a special train from Maidstone West to Chatham Dockyard on 1st April 1993 to consider the use of steam on the line again as part of the Chatham Historical Dockyard project. (J.H.Aston)

93. The Dockyard closed in 1984, the Royal Navy having used it since the yard was established by King Henry VIII in 1560. As many of the buildings were of national importance, the western part of the yard was set aside as an 80-acre site to show the history of ship building and much else. Although dieselised, the yard retained this one steam locomotive to the end. It is Robert Stephenson & Hawthorn 0-4-0ST *Ajax* and it is seen alongside the Southern Electric Group's DEMU railtour on 20th April 1985. (A.Dasi-Sutton)

94. The North Downs Steam Railway steam-hauled two ex-LT Underground coaches on the site in the 1985 season but the NDSR eventually settled at Stone and the coaches went to Alderney. When photographed in April 1994 only these and a few other wagons remained on site, plus a number of industrial diesel locomotives and *Ajax*. They were in use occasionally. (V.Mitchell)

95. Another 1994 photograph includes a dual gauge weighbridge installed in one of the seven covered slips in 1915. The slips in some of these shipbuilding sheds have been infilled and the structures now house a wide variety of historic transport items, ranging from submarines to steam lorries. A splendid opportunity exists to operate historic tramcars (with on-board modern generators) on the extensive track-work remaining and thus reduce visitor exhaustion on the large site. (V.Mitchell)

96. Before building work could take place on the less historic parts of the Dockyard, over 600,000 tons of contaminated soil had to be removed in sealed containers. One is being loaded onto a flat wagon on 15th February 1992. The sidings were located near the middle of the 1947 Admiralty chart, the one on the left being for cripples. (J.A.M.Vaughan)

97. A few minutes after the last picture was taken the same locomotive begins its slog up the gradient to Gillingham. Parts of this LCDR pattern signal may date from the 1880s. The low-level spectacles would be useful in fog - they were electrically lit. The line was taken out of use in July 1993. (J.A.M.Vaughan)

98. A week later, no.33042 was recorded nearer Gillingham with six wagons of waste bound for Hoo Junction Yard. Here they were marshalled into trains of 16 bogies for conveyance to a former brickworks pit at Stewartby in Bedfordshire. English transport history was being made in the background with the construction of the country's first immersed tube road tunnel. Britain's first was under the Conwy in Wales. (J.A.M.Vaughan)

RAINHAM

99. The station opened on 25th January 1858 as "Rainham & Newington" but the suffix was dropped in 1862 when a station was opened at that place. Included in this view is the goods shed and a boat race poster dated 1st April 1912. (Lens of Sutton)

100. The down refuge siding is evident as class D1 no. 31505 proceeds east on 15th June 1957 with the 11.50am Victoria to Dover Priory. The train has passed over three level crossings (Beechings, Tyndall and Smarts), none of which now exists. (J.H.Aston)

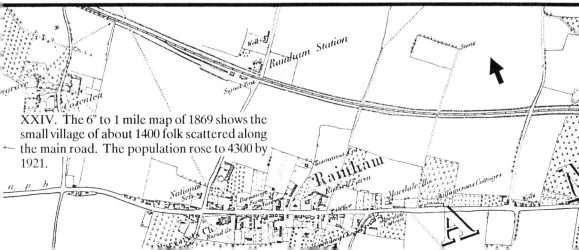

XXIV. The 6" to 1 mile map of 1869 shows the small village of about 1400 folk scattered along the main road. The population rose to 4300 by 1921.

101. Cars are parking in the goods yard which closed on 2nd April 1962. The goods shed contained a hand worked crane of 35cwt. capacity. (British Rail)

XXV. 1878 edition. There were no sidings here when the line opened.

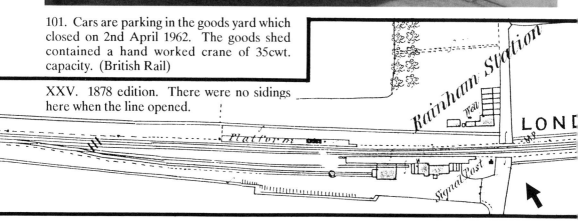

102. Another view from the 1960s includes a newspaper stall in an exposed position beyond the house. (British Rail)

103. A 1977 photograph includes the replacement footbridge, the lengthened platform for 12-car trains and the featureless CLASP building. A prefabricated concrete footbridge had been erected by the level crossing in 1926. (N.D.Mundy)

104. The CLASP structure was replaced by one with some style in 1990. CCTV therein and treated surfaces have reduced vandalism. The signal box replaced one on the other side of the track on 26th April 1959 and controlled barriers were introduced on 17th December 1972. The train is the 06.44 Liverpool to Dover Western Docks, hauled by no. 47825 on 15th September 1992. (J.Scrace)

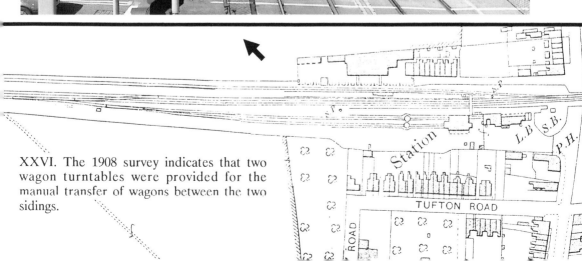

XXVI. The 1908 survey indicates that two wagon turntables were provided for the manual transfer of wagons between the two sidings.

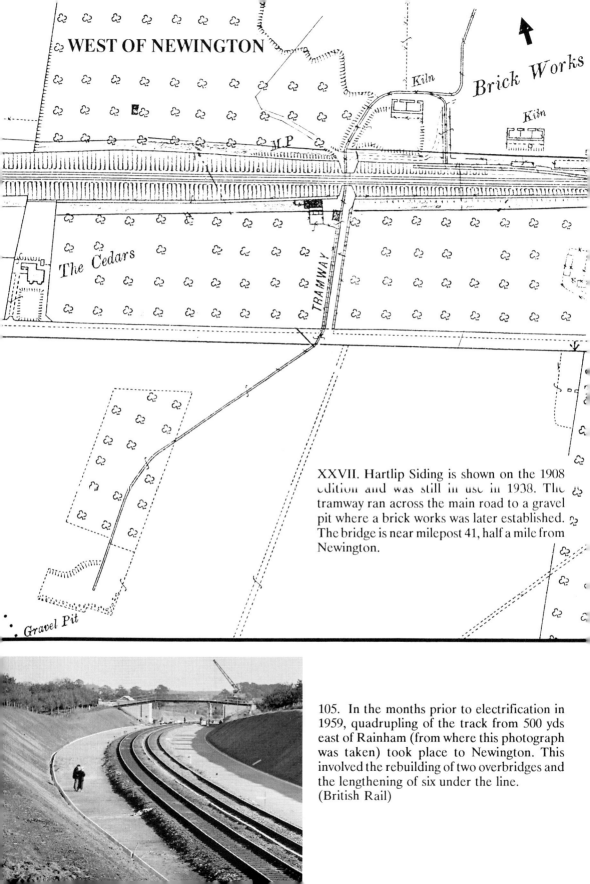

WEST OF NEWINGTON

Kiln

Brick Works

Kiln

M.P

The Cedars

TRAMWAY

XXVII. Hartlip Siding is shown on the 1908 edition and was still in use in 1938. The tramway ran across the main road to a gravel pit where a brick works was later established. The bridge is near milepost 41, half a mile from Newington.

Gravel Pit

105. In the months prior to electrification in 1959, quadrupling of the track from 500 yds east of Rainham (from where this photograph was taken) took place to Newington. This involved the rebuilding of two overbridges and the lengthening of six under the line.
(British Rail)

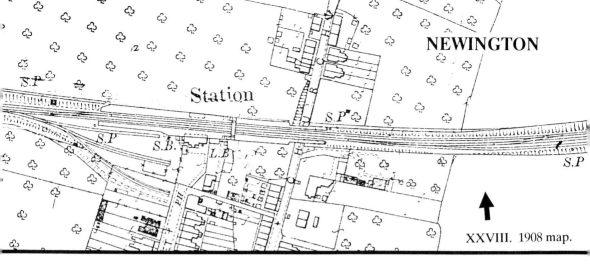

NEWINGTON

XXVIII. 1908 map.

106. Opened on 1st August 1862, the station served a community of only 850 people but there was traffic to be had from the local orchards and farms. This eastward view shows that there was also advertising revenue to be had. (Lens of Sutton)

107. During the quadrupling the up platform was raised and lengthened, also the points to the goods yard were moved 100yds westward. The signal box remained in use until 26th April 1959 when Rainham Panel took over and all four tracks came into use. (Lens of Sutton)

108. LMS-designed 2-6-2T no.41212 stands at one of the two temporary platforms erected during the widening work. Behind the up

platform, vans stand in the goods yard which closed on 1st October 1962. (British Rail)

109. The new footbridge and the replacement station buildings were photographed in September 1992. The quadruple section is just over two miles in length. (J.Scrace)

WEST OF SITTINGBOURNE

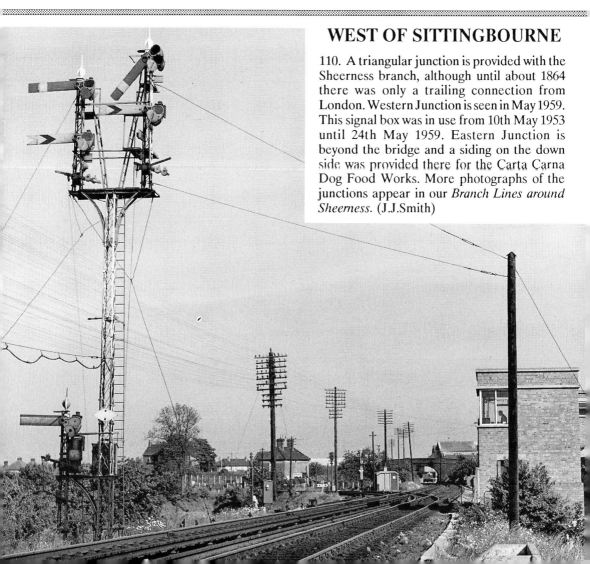

110. A triangular junction is provided with the Sheerness branch, although until about 1864 there was only a trailing connection from London. Western Junction is seen in May 1959. This signal box was in use from 10th May 1953 until 24th May 1959. Eastern Junction is beyond the bridge and a siding on the down side was provided there for the Carta Carna Dog Food Works. More photographs of the junctions appear in our *Branch Lines around Sheerness*. (J.J.Smith)

SITTINGBOURNE

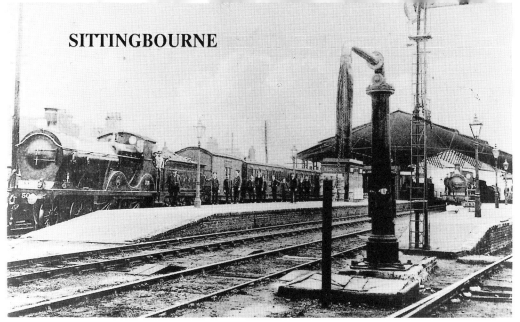

111. The station opened with the line and was graced with an overall roof in 1863. Trains started to run to Sheerness in 1860 and a loop line with platform was provided for them. Class E no.506 of 1905 is seen at this platform. (Lens of Sutton)

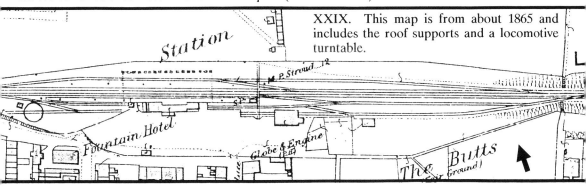

XXIX. This map is from about 1865 and includes the roof supports and a locomotive turntable.

112. A covered footbridge replaced the previous subway which was infilled. The roof over the tracks survived until 1952 but the roof on the footbridge still existed in 1994. (D.Cullum coll.)

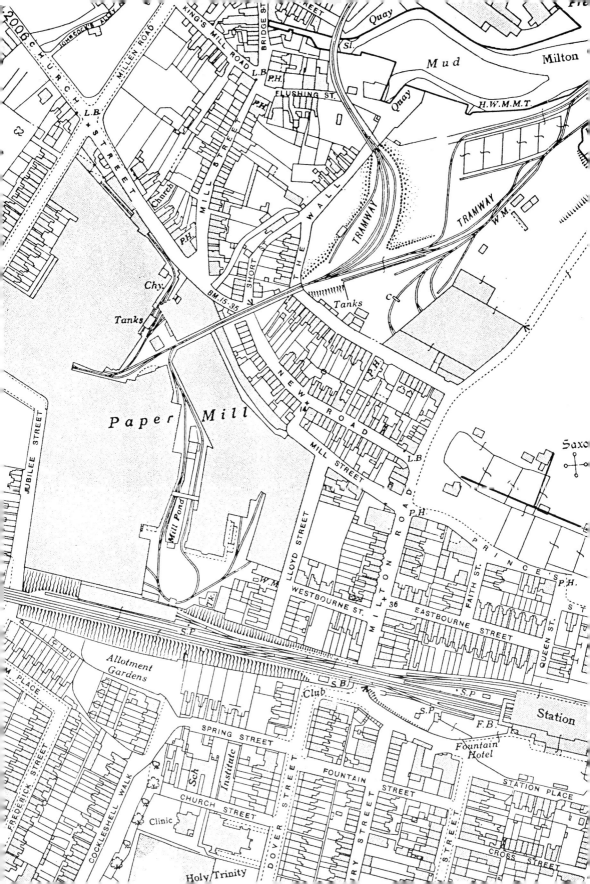

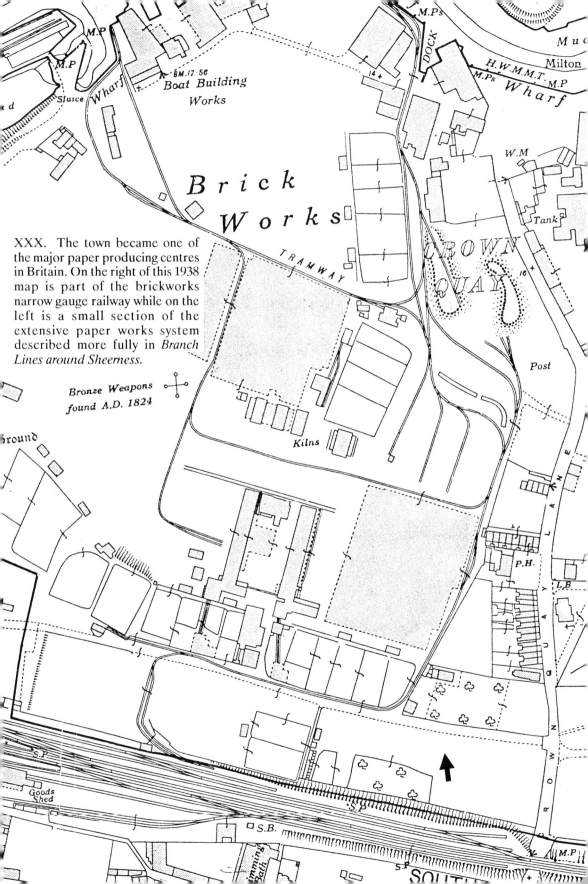

XXX. The town became one of the major paper producing centres in Britain. On the right of this 1938 map is part of the brickworks narrow gauge railway while on the left is a small section of the extensive paper works system described more fully in *Branch Lines around Sheerness*.

Bronze Weapons found A.D. 1824

Boat Building Works

Brick Works

TRAMWAY

Kilns

CROWN QUAY

Post

Wharf

Sluice

Dock

Milton

Tank

W.M

P.H.

L.B

Goods Shed

S.P

S.B.

SOUTH

113. The 2ft 6in gauge railway to the paper works was operated by Bowaters until 1969 when part of it was set aside for preservation. Part of the elevated line near the works is seen in 1974 with 0-4-2 ST *Premier* in action. (F.Hornby)

114. Included in this westward view are "A" Box, a carriage siding, the paper work's covered siding and spacious facilities for gentlemen. Both signal boxes were replaced by a new one at the east end of the station on 24th May 1959. (Lens of Sutton)

115. The short dock siding was still in use when the 5.17pm Dover Priory to Gillingham was photographed on 15th June 1957 in perfect lighting conditions. At night, gas light still prevailed. No. 31781 was of class L and was built in Germany in 1914. (P.Hay)

Other pictures and maps of this station are included in the companion albums *Sittingbourne to Ramsgate* **and** *Branch Lines around Sheerness.*

116. Platform lengthening and improvement was in progress as class L no. 31766 departed east on 19th July 1958. The gleaming coaches are of Bulleid's design; the leading one includes a periscope to enable the guard to check signals. (D.Trevor Rowe)

117. Conductor rails are in position as an N class 2-6-0 arrives on 18th May 1959. The goods yard was open to public traffic until 5th July 1976, one van being visible on the left. The platform canopies date from 1952. (A.E.Bennett)

118. Both canopies were removed in 1986 as part of a major renovation scheme. They were replaced by an equally incompatible glazed structure but at least this important building still stands. (C.Hall)

119. No.47258 stands in the down goods loop on 5th July 1992, with liquid oxygen wagons attached. This commodity is used by Sheerness Steels in their smelting process. The conductor rail in this loop was de-energised that year but the Sheerness passenger train frequency was doubled to two per hour in the following year. (F.Hornby)

120. Another unusual traffic to be seen in 1993 was starch, up to 50 wagons arriving each month from Manchester. The paper industry also received even larger quantities of liquid china clay and chalk slurry at the shed seen in the background of picture no.114. (V.Mitchell)

MP Middleton Press

Easebourne Lane, Midhurst. West Sussex. GU29 9AZ   Tel: (0730) 813169 Fax: (0730) 812601
..... Write or telephone for our latest list .....

BRANCH LINES

Branch Line to Allhallows
Branch Lines to Alton
Branch Lines tround Ascot
Branch Line to Bude
Branch Lines to East Grinstead
Branch Lines tround Effingham Jn
Branch Lines to Exmouth
Branch Line to Fairford
Branch Lines around Gosport
Branch Line to Hawkhurst
Branch Line to Hayling
Branch Lines to Horsham
Branch Lines around Huntingdon
Branch Lines to Ilfracombe
Branch Lines to Longmoor
Branch Line to Lyme Regis
Branch Line to Lynton
Branch Lines around March
Branch Lines around Midhurst
Branch Line to Minehead
Branch Lines to Newport
Branch Lines around Portmadoc 1923-46
Branch Lines around Porthmadog 1954-94
Branch Lines to Seaton & Sidmouth
Branch Line to Selsey
Branch Lines around Sheerness
Branch Line to Shrewsbury
Branch Line to Southwold
Branch Line to Swanage
Branch Line to Tenterden
Branch Lines to Tunbridge Wells
Branch Lines tround Weymouth
Branch Lines around Wimborne

LONDON SUBURBAN RAILWAYS

Caterham and Tattenham Corner
Charing Cross to Dartford
Crystal Palace and Catford Loop
Holborn Viaduct to Lewisham
Kingston and Hounslow Loops
Lewisham to Dartford
London Bridge to Addiscombe
Mitcham Junction Lines
West Croydon to Epsom

STEAMING THROUGH

Steaming through Cornwall
Steaming through East Sussex
Steaming through the Isle of Wight
Steaming through Surrey
Steaming through West Hants
Steaming through West Sussex

SOUTH COAST RAILWAYS

Ashford to Dover
Bournemouth to Weymouth
Brighton to Eastbourne
Brighton to Worthing
Chichester to Portsmouth
Dover to Ramsgate
Eastbourne to Hastings
Hastings to Ashford
Ryde to Ventnor
Southampton to Bournemouth

SOUTHERN MAIN LINES

Basingstoke to Salisbury
Bromley South to Rochester
Charing Cross to Orpington
Crawley to Littlehampton
Dartford to Sittingbourne
East Croydon to Three Bridges
Epsom to Horsham
Exeter to Barnstaple
Faversham to Dover
Haywards Heath to Seaford
London Bridge to East Croydon
Orpington to Tonbridge
Salisbury to Yeovil
Sittingbourne to Ramsgate
Three Bridges to Brighton
Tonbridge to Hastings
Victoria to Bromley South
Waterloo to Windsor
Waterloo to Woking
Woking to Southampton
Yeovil to Exeter

COUNTRY RAILWAY ROUTES

Andover to Southampton
Bath To Evercreech Junction
Bournemouth to Evercreech Jn
Burnham to Evercreech Junction
East Kent Light Railway
Fareham to Salisbury
Guildford to Redhill
Reading to Basingstoke
Reading to Guildford
Redhill to Ashford
Strood to Paddock Wood
Woking to Alton

SOUTHERN RAILWAY VIDEO

War on the Line

TRAMWAY CLASSICS

Brighton's Tramways
Camberwell & W. Norwood Tramway
Dover's Tramways
Exeter & Taunton Tramways
Greenwich & Dartford Tramways
Hastings Tramways
Lewisham & Catford Tramways
Southampton Tramways
Southend-on-sea Tramways
Thanet's Tramways

BUS BOOKS

Eastbourne Bus Story
Tillingbourne Bus Story

OTHER RAILWAY BOOKS

Garraway Father & Son
Industrial Railways of the South East
London Chatham & Dover Railway
South Eastern Railway
War on the Line

MILITARY BOOKS

Battle Over Portsmouth
Battle Over Sussex 1940
Military Defence of West Sussex

WATERWAY ALBUMS

Hampshire Waterways
Kent and East Sussex Waterways
West Sussex Waterways

COUNTRY BOOKS

Brickmaking in Sussex
East Grinstead Then and Now
Leigh Park
Walking Ashdown Forest